500 Mystery Murder Scenes For Writers

Includes The Amazing Murder Scene Generator!

Create Thousands Of Mystery Murder Story Ideas!

IRIN BLACKBURN

CONTENTS

DISCLAIMER

This is a work of fiction. Names, characters, businesses, places, events and incidents are either the products of the author's imagination or used in a fictitious manner. Any resemblance to actual persons, living or dead, or actual events is purely coincidental.

INTRODUCTION

Get ready to be inspired by 500 murder scenes and murder mystery ideas in this book!

Which story will you tell?

Simply pick a murder scene in this book and let your imagination write the rest of the story. Will you write a tale of long-held grudges, a revenge killing, a crime of passion or just a good old fashioned psychopathic murder? Whatever brilliant story you choose to write, this book is the perfect tool to help you brainstorm new stories, novels, screenplays and scripts.

But that's not all. You are not just limited to just 500 murder scene ideas with this book.

The Amazing Murder Scene Generator at the end of the book allows you to create thousands of different murder scenes and story ideas. It lets you randomly combine four to five different elements to generate a unique murder scene. With hundreds of scene settings, characters and personal conflicts for you to play around with, the murder story possibilities are endless.

And now, the curtain rises on yet another murder... On to the murder scene ideas!

MURDER SCENES #1 - 100

Murder Scene #1

Where: The victim was found in a private swimming pool
How: Attacked by piranhas
Who: A sexy administrative assistant who was having an affair with her boss
Detail: There is a deep cut on the victim's lips

Murder Scene #2

Where: The body was found under a tree
How: Poisoned rosary
Who: A religious leader who was disfigured in a terrible accident years ago
Detail: The victim held a torn photograph in his hand

Murder Scene #3

Where: The deceased was found in a cargo crate in an airplane
How: Bitten by a puff adder
Who: A foreign language interpreter who is not what he seemed to be
Detail: There is a strand of hair in the victim's hand

Murder Scene #4

Where: The body was found in a private girls' school
How: Stabbed in the eye with a knitting needle
Who: A belligerent school mistress
Detail: Someone saw the victim in an unexpected place before she died

Murder Scene #5

Where: The body was found hanging from a window
How: Bitten to death by army ants
Who: A veterinarian with a dark family past
Detail: The victim had received something unusual in the mail before he died

Murder Scene #6

Where: The deceased was found in a brothel
How: Fatal allergic reaction to latex in a condom

Who: A senator involved in shady business
Detail: The victim's wedding ring is missing

Murder Scene #7

Where: The victim was found in a sewer
How: Eaten alive by rats
Who: A fashion model who had undergone plastic surgery
Detail: The victim was wearing heels that do not belong to her

Murder Scene #8

Where: The victim was found in a concrete mixer
How: Signs of being buried alive in concrete
Who: A suave salesman with a reputation for womanizing
Detail: The victim's shirt pocket was ripped off

Murder Scene #9

Where: The victim was found in the sewer
How: Burnt alive with kerosene
Who: A door to door salesman who is an alcoholic
Detail: The victim had left behind a bizarre message on his mobile phone

Murder Scene #10

Where: The victim was found on the railroad tracks
How: Dragged to death on the rails behind a moving train
Who: An obsessive railroad inspector who keeps to himself
Detail: A piano wire is found on the scene.

Murder Scene #11

Where: The body was found in a top secret laboratory
How: Bitten by a yellow sac spider
Who: An outspoken animal scientist
Detail: The victim's ankles were duct taped together

Murder Scene #12

Where: The deceased was found in a car park
How: Injection with poison from an umbrella
Who: An arrogant diplomat with a penchant for vintage cars

Detail: There was no sign of a struggle

Murder Scene #13

Where: The deceased was found near a jogging path
How: Fatal allergic reaction to pollen
Who: A disgruntled pharmacy aide about to expose a corporation
Detail: A witness saw the victim having an intense conversation with someone

Murder Scene #14

Where: The deceased was found inside a gym locker room
How: Poisoned gym towel
Who: A possessive football star
Detail: A witness has tampered with the murder scene

Murder Scene #15

Where: The deceased was found in an opera theatre
How: Crushed by a falling chandelier
Who: A spy who was holding onto an important document
Detail: There is a white substance on the victim's fingers

Murder Scene #16

Where: The body was found at the bottom of a well
How: Strangled to death with a wedding veil
Who: A runaway bride
Detail: The murderer had an accomplice

Murder Scene #17

Where: The body was found in a gun firing range
How: Strangled with a thin wire
Who: A secretary about to expose her boss
Detail: The victim had unexplainable bruises on her forearm

Murder Scene #18

Where: The deceased was found in a dry swimming pool
How: Broken neck from a great fall
Who: A teenage cheerleader who was being threatened

Detail: The victim's clothes are wet

Murder Scene #19

Where: The body was found in a dumpster behind a restaurant
How: Strangled by a belt
Who: An abusive criminal lawyer who was hiding something that happened two decades ago
Detail: There are strange cuts on the victim's legs

Murder Scene #20

Where: The deceased was found on a luxury yacht
How: A gunshot wound in the chest
Who: A perfectionist diver with a mysterious past
Detail: The victim has a red line on her forehead

Murder Scene #21

Where: The deceased was found in a car workshop
How: Fatal allergic reaction to fumes
Who: An advertising executive who was having a love affair
Detail: There are strange marks on the victim's hands

Murder Scene #22

Where: The deceased was found at the entrance of a university
How: Run over by a car
Who: A compulsive athletic coach covering up for somebody
Detail: A witness heard the victim scolding someone

Murder Scene #23

Where: The victim was found in a train cabin
How: Poisoned wine glass
Who: An opinionated aeronautical engineer
Detail: Something is abnormal about the victim's fingers

Murder Scene #24

Where: The deceased was found in a university lecture hall
How: Struck on the head by a falling podium
Who: A school administrator about to retrench the teaching staff

Detail: Something is missing from the victim's desk

Murder Scene #25

Where: The body was found in a train station terminal
How: Stabbed in the stomach with an icepick
Who: A biomedical engineer in heavy debt
Detail: There is adhesive residue on the victim's fingertips

Murder Scene #26

Where: The deceased was found in the street
How: Struck on the head by a falling brick
Who: A biological technician who has a strange habit
Detail: The victim's home was ransacked

Murder Scene #27

Where: The victim was found in a music studio
How: Head bashed in with a guitar
Who: A media mogul with intense rivalries at work
Detail: A witness is lying about something

Murder Scene #28

Where: The deceased was found in a school storeroom
How: Strangled by a shoelace
Who: A popular physical education teacher
Detail: The room was locked from the inside

Murder Scene #29

Where: The body was found in a river bed
How: Struck on the throat with a cleaver
Who: An office clerk who has relationship problems
Detail: Something is wrong with the victim's estimated time of death

Murder Scene #30

Where: The deceased was found in a public washroom
How: Strangled by pantyhose
Who: A rugby star in the middle of a sex scandal
Detail: The victim's water was drugged

Murder Scene #31

Where: The victim was found underwater in a marine tourist attraction
How: Broken neck as a whale pulled his head underwater
Who: An marine animal trainer hiding something
Detail: Something is missing from the victim's belongings

Murder Scene #32

Where: The body was found in a hotel toilet
How: Struck on the head by a heavy toilet tank lid
Who: A brilliant opera tenor who lied about his past
Detail: A glove is missing from the victim's hand

Murder Scene #33

Where: The deceased was found splayed on a museum exhibit
How: Stabbed in the chest with an antique sword
Who: A museum curator who was involved in a domestic abuse case some years ago
Detail: The victim's ankle has a thin red thread around it

Murder Scene #34

Where: The deceased was found in a church
How: Bitten by a redback spider
Who: A priest who was leading double lives
Detail: A broken off key was found at the crime scene

Murder Scene #35

Where: The deceased was found in the passenger seat of a car
How: Carbon monoxide poisoning
Who: A conceited journalist who was about to release a big story
Detail: There is something strange about the victim's collar

Murder Scene #36

Where: The body was found on a hotel roof
How: Struck on the head with a hammer
Who: An ambitious radio news commentator
Detail: There was a hastily written note stuffed in the victim's pocket

Murder Scene #37

Where: The body was found on the roof of a community school
How: Choked to death on ball bearings
Who: An adult literacy teacher who was acquitted from a crime some years ago
Detail: The victim's notebook pages are all torn out

Murder Scene #38

Where: The body was found in a garden shed
How: Stung to death by hornets
Who: An entertainment agent who was two-timing her boyfriend
Detail: The victim's hair band is missing

Murder Scene #39

Where: The body was found in an abandoned car on a dirt road
How: Head struck by a baseball bat
Who: A teenage pop idol with enemies in the entertainment scene
Detail: The victim's hands were tied to the steering wheel

Murder Scene #40

Where: The deceased was found in a bedroom of an upscale condominium
How: Clobbered to death with a bathroom scale
Who: A popular TV talk host who was about to resign
Detail: There is a small cut on the victim's cheek

Murder Scene #41

Where: The deceased was found in an underground bunker
How: Throat slit by a wire
Who: A fearful government intelligence specialist hiding from somebody
Detail: Someone had videotaped the murder

Murder Scene #42

Where: The victim was found inside a air hangar
How: Multiple injuries in head from a drill
Who: An ostentatious air pilot who likes to brag
Detail: The victim's eyes were dilated

Murder Scene #43

Where: The body was found on a couch of an office
How: Poisoned bandaid
Who: A childcare worker who lied about his past
Detail: There is a strong scent in the crime scene

Murder Scene #44

Where: The body was found in a fridge
How: Struck on the head by a heavy ashtray
Who: An egoistical fashion designer about to break into the limelight
Detail: There are red spots on the victim's neck

Murder Scene #45

Where: The victim was found in a coffee shop
How: Poisoned mug
Who: An aggressive insurance agent who blew the whistle on her employer
Detail: The victim's mobile phone has a secret message

Murder Scene #46

Where: The victim was found at the seashore
How: Bludgeoned to death with a crowbar
Who: A casting director on the brink of casting an actress for a film role
Detail: A witness saw the victim meeting with an unexpected person

Murder Scene #47

Where: The deceased was found at a landfill
How: Crushed to death in a waste compactor
Who: A suave financial analyst who was blackmailing somebody
Detail: Someone witnessed the victim tearing up an envelope furiously

Murder Scene #48

Where: The deceased was found in a field of wheat
How: Throat slit by broken glass
Who: A foreign service officer who betrayed her country
Detail: There is an odd lipstick smudge at the victim's neck

Murder Scene #49

Where: The victim was found in a hotel room
How: Strangled by a bra strap
Who: A ruthless politician
Detail: A witness noticed the victim behaving secretively the day before

Murder Scene #50

Where: The body was found in the living room of an apartment
How: Crushed to death by a toppling refrigerator
Who: A famed medical professor about to release a research paper
Detail: The victim's mobile phone has a secret message

Murder Scene #51

Where: The deceased was found in a hair salon
How: Stabbed in the eye with a pair of scissors
Who: A shy hairdresser who had seen something she shouldn't
Detail: The victim's watch is missing

Murder Scene #52

Where: The body was found in a restaurant
How: Fatal allergic reaction to shellfish
Who: A flirtatious television personality who was blackmailing somebody
Detail: There is something odd about the cutlery on the table

Murder Scene #53

Where: The deceased was found in a posh mansion
How: Drowned in a toilet bowl
Who: A CID special agent with a secret
Detail: The room of the crime scene was unusually hot

Murder Scene #54

Where: The deceased was found in a lake
How: Dismembered alive by machete
Who: A detective with a secret obsession
Detail: A witness saw the victim chasing after someone

Murder Scene #55

Where: The deceased was found on a car racing track
How: Burnt to death with petrol
Who: A well-known race driver who was planning to flee the country that night
Detail: The lock to the victim's home was broken

Murder Scene #56

Where: The deceased was found in a bath tub
How: Electrocution
Who: A real estate broker cheating on his wife
Detail: The victim's wrist watch stopped at midnight

Murder Scene #57

Where: The deceased was found in a club
How: Stabbed in the head with a sharp stiletto shoe
Who: An award-winning art director having multiple love affairs
Detail: The victim's hair is wet

Murder Scene #58

Where: The victim was found encased inside a block of cement
How: Struck on the head with a golf club
Who: A domineering steel magnate going through a divorce
Detail: The murderer has left a clue behind on the victim's skin

Murder Scene #59

Where: The deceased was found in a lift lobby
How: Mercury poisoning
Who: A prominent human rights activist about to reveal something to the press
Detail: A missing key to a safe is involved

Murder Scene #60

Where: The body was found in a garden shed
How: Strangled by a dog leash
Who: An arrogant film starlet
Detail: The victim's fingernails have an unidentified substance underneath

them

Murder Scene #61

Where: The body was found in a publishing house
How: Stabbed in the neck several times with a pen
Who: A timid editorial writer
Detail: The victim's hands were tied together with cable ties

Murder Scene #62

Where: The body was found hidden inside a bale of straw on a farm
How: Gored by hogs on the farm
Who: A rancher who is going to sell off the farm
Detail: There is a bloody thumbprint on the victim's belt

Murder Scene #63

Where: The deceased was found in a cooking vat
How: Stabbed in the eye with a steak knife
Who: An restaurant owner with a secret
Detail: The victim's home was ransacked

Murder Scene #64

Where: The deceased was found in a playground
How: Decapitated by a wire
Who: An over-zealous police officer who does something odd every week
Detail: A witness had overheard a strange conversation

Murder Scene #65

Where: The deceased was found in a fast food outlet
How: Fatal allergic reaction to eggs
Who: A record producer with a gambling problem
Detail: A witness had seen the victim behaving fearfully the day he died

Murder Scene #66

Where: The body was found in the basement of a house
How: Suffocated by kitty litter
Who: An computer programmer who was engaged in corporate espionage
Detail: The victim's hand seemed to be pointing at something

Murder Scene #67

Where: The victim was found in a bathroom
How: Poisoned toothbrush
Who: A corrupt law judge
Detail: The victim's fingernails have an unidentified substance underneath them

Murder Scene #68

Where: The body was found in a carpark
How: Shot in the head by a nailgun
Who: A military analyst who was holding onto an important document
Detail: A witness overheard the victim having an angry phone conversation with someone

Murder Scene #69

Where: The body was found in a meat packing factory
How: Crushed to death by falling meat carcasses
Who: A meat packer who does something peculiar every afternoon
Detail: The victim was going to reveal something important to a witness before he died

Murder Scene #70

Where: The victim was found in a kennel
How: Suffocated to death by a python
Who: A housewife with a dark secret
Detail: There is something strange about the victim's clothing

Murder Scene #71

Where: The deceased was found under a bridge
How: Crushed to death by an avalanche of trash
Who: A peace corps worker facing a lawsuit
Detail: The victim was wearing only one contact lens

Murder Scene #72

Where: The deceased was found in the basement
How: Struck on the head by a manual typewriter

Who: A famous novelist with a jealous rival
Detail: There was red ink all over the victim's hands

Murder Scene #73

Where: The body was found in an animal shelter
How: Attacked by dogs in the animal shelter
Who: A brash animal shelter worker about to expose his boss
Detail: The murder took place in the heat of summer

Murder Scene #74

Where: The victim was found in a hotel corridor
How: Methanol poisoning
Who: An politician with a dark past
Detail: The soles of the victim's shoes are muddy

Murder Scene #75

Where: The deceased was found in an underground tunnel
How: Burnt to death with a blow torch
Who: An ex-CIA agent
Detail: A witness has tampered with the murder scene

Murder Scene #76

Where: The body was found in a flour mill
How: Crushed by a falling sandbag
Who: A mill worker who was spying on someone
Detail: The victim's hands are wet

Murder Scene #77

Where: The deceased was found in the bathroom
How: Throat cut by shattered glass from a shower door
Who: A famous TV and radio personality
Detail: The blood splatters on the walls do not match up

Murder Scene #78

Where: The deceased was found on the floor of a stock exchange
How: Strangled by a computer mouse cord
Who: A stock broker who was hiding something that happened two

decades ago
Detail: The victm's shoes were placed neatly twenty feet away from the body

Murder Scene #79

Where: The victim was found in a bakery
How: Suffocated with dough stuffed down the throat
Who: Bakery worker
Detail: The victim's work apron was swapped

Murder Scene #80

Where: The victim was found at the entrance of his gated community
How: Crushed to death by an electronic gate
Who: A secretive bank manager who was being investigated for fraud
Detail: The victim had hurried out of the house after receiving a strange phone call

Murder Scene #81

Where: The body was found at a luxury resort
How: Poisoned BBQ skewers
Who: A fashion magazine editor with jealous rivals
Detail: A thumb drive is missing from the victim's handbag

Murder Scene #82

Where: The body was found on the roof of a high school
How: Strangled by a braid of hair
Who: A school nurse with a secret obsession
Detail: The victim was trying to reach something

Murder Scene #83

Where: The deceased was found in a walk-in freezer
How: Fatal allergic reaction to peanuts
Who: Teenage daughter of a shipping tycoon
Detail: There are red scars on the victim's neck

Murder Scene #84

Where: The victim was found inside a church

How: Fatal allergic reaction to pollen
Who: A wedding bride
Detail: A witness saw someone tampering with the bridal bouquet

Murder Scene #85

Where: The body was found in a school bowling alley
How: Struck on the head by a bowling ball
Who: A high school teacher who was having a love affair with a student
Detail: The victim died in an unusual pose

Murder Scene #86

Where: The body was found in a luxurious penthouse
How: Clobbered to death with a toaster
Who: A rich heiress living with her musician boyfriend
Detail: The victim had scratched a message before she died

Murder Scene #87

Where: The deceased was found in a gym locker
How: Dismembered alive by axe
Who: A compulsive criminal lawyer
Detail: A tattoo on the victim's arm may provide a clue to the murderer's identity

Murder Scene #88

Where: The deceased was found in the office pantry
How: Poisoned mustard
Who: A cardiologist who was an important court witness
Detail: A witness saw the victim exchanging suitcases with someone on the street

Murder Scene #89

Where: The deceased was found on an apartment balcony
How: Struck on the head by a boomerang
Who: A divorce lawyer involved in a high profile case
Detail: The victim received an odd message on her mobile phone before she died

Murder Scene #90

Where: The body was found in an animal cage
How: Kicked to death by zebras
Who: A zoologist with a strange habit
Detail: The hard disk of the victim's laptop has been erased

Murder Scene #91

Where: The deceased was found in a fish market
How: Suffocated with a large fish forced down the throat
Who: A highly respected sushi chef
Detail: The back of the victim's neck is sticky with something

Murder Scene #92

Where: The body was found in an attic bedroom
How: Toxic wallpaper
Who: A novelist about to release his first book
Detail: A witness saw the victim in a dispute with someone

Murder Scene #93

Where: The deceased was found in the bedroom of an apartment
How: Suffocated to death by a vacuum cleaner in the mouth
Who: A housekeeper with a fetish
Detail: The victim was tied to the bed

Murder Scene #94

Where: The deceased was found in the driver seat of a limousine
How: Poisoned gloves
Who: A limousine chauffeur
Detail: The victim had complained of someone stalking him

Murder Scene #95

Where: The body was found in a fun ride in the amusement park
How: Poison needle
Who: Niece of a steel magnate who is embroiled in a will dispute
Detail: A witness overheard the victim having an angry phone conversation with someone

Murder Scene #96

Where: The deceased was found in a wax musuem
How: Died from injuries consistent with a car crash
Who: A beautiful teenage fashion model
Detail: There is a needle mark on the victim's neck

Murder Scene #97

Where: The body was found hanging in a waterfall
How: Stung to death by fire ants
Who: A cocky forest biologist who keeps odd hours
Detail: The victim's feet were tied together

Murder Scene #98

Where: The body was found in a theatre dressing room
How: Toxic makeup containing arsenic
Who: An award-winning actress who was involved in a scandal with a politician
Detail: The victim's bodice has a faint stain on it

Murder Scene #99

Where: The deceased was found in a public library
How: Poisoned bookmark
Who: A mild librarian who saw something he was not supposed to see
Detail: The victim's glasses are missing

Murder Scene #100

Where: The victim was found in an office
How: Fatal allergic reaction to perfume
Who: A famous television script writer
Detail: Someone saw the victim dashing out of her office

MURDER SCENES #101 - 200

Murder Scene #101

Where: The victim was found in an airplane
How: Poisoned airline food
Who: A pompous travel writer who lied to her employers
Detail: A witness heard the victim bragging about something

Murder Scene #102

Where: The victim was found in a dentist's chair
How: Poisoned dental instrument
Who: A drug kingpin with a strange habit
Detail: There is something strange about the victim's socks

Murder Scene #103

Where: The body was found at the bottom of an elevator shaft
How: Air bubble in the artery
Who: A music industry executive who was involved in a scandal with a singer
Detail: There is a cut on the victim's neck

Murder Scene #104

Where: The victim was found in the washroom of a bar
How: Toxic underwear
Who: An nun who had undergone plastic surgery
Detail: The victim's niece received something in the mail from the victim before she died

Murder Scene #105

Where: The body was found in an all-boys boarding school
How: Stabbed in the throat with a pocket knife
Who: A strict school administrator with a grudge
Detail: The victim's watch is missing

Murder Scene #106

Where: The body was found by a lamp post
How: Thallium sulfate poisoning

Who: A ballerina who had seen something she shouldn't
Detail: There is an unidentified powder on the victim's wrist

Murder Scene #107

Where: The deceased was found on stage
How: Fatally injured with a stage prop weapon that turned out to be real
Who: An award winning theatre actor
Detail: The victim received a mysterious voice recording before he died

Murder Scene #108

Where: The victim was found in a van
How: Throat torn out by what seems to a large animal bite
Who: An obstinate restaurant cook with money issues
Detail: There are strange cuts on the victim's legs

Murder Scene #109

Where: The deceased was found in a schoolyard
How: Throat cut by a broken DVD
Who: A well regarded preschool teacher
Detail: There is a blue stain on the victim's coat

Murder Scene #110

Where: The victim was found in the deep woods
How: Suffocated to death with nose and mouth sealed by industrial strength glue
Who: A combat engineer who lied about something
Detail: The victim was trying to reach something

Murder Scene #111

Where: The body was found in a luxury home
How: Stabbed in the eye with a knife
Who: A well-respected interior designer facing a divorce
Detail: The lock to the victim's home was broken

Murder Scene #112

Where: The deceased was found in a cruise ship
How: Blowfish poisoning

Who: An aristocrat with a perverse hobby
Detail: A stash of secret photos was found in the victim's home

Murder Scene #113

Where: The body was found inside a hotel room
How: Lead poisoning
Who: A computer programmer with a shady past
Detail: The murderer had an accomplice

Murder Scene #114

Where: The victim was found in a refuse dump
How: Poisoned by antifreeze
Who: A commodities trader with a secret
Detail: The victim's home was burned to the ground

Murder Scene #115

Where: The body was found by a dirt road
How: Beaten to death
Who: A teenage girl who was spying on someone
Detail: There is something in the victim's mouth

Murder Scene #116

Where: The deceased was found hanging from a crane
How: Thallium sulfate poisoning
Who: A chief financial officer about to retrench his staff
Detail: The victim was blindfolded

Murder Scene #117

Where: The deceased was found under a bridge
How: Bitten to death by wild dogs
Who: A harsh refuse collector who found something suspicious
Detail: The victim has a black mark on his temple

Murder Scene #118

Where: The victim was found in a tar pit
How: Struck on the head with a heavy walking cane
Who: An espionage intelligence agent who was on the run

Detail: A lipstick mark was found on the victim's shirt

Murder Scene #119

Where: The victim was found inside an antique cabinet
How: Nicotine poisoning
Who: An elderly clergy member who overheard a secret
Detail: The victim's hand seemed to be pointing at something

Murder Scene #120

Where: The body was found in the carpark
How: Fatal sting from scorpion
Who: A marriage therapist being blackmailed
Detail: There was a receipt in the victim's pocket

Murder Scene #121

Where: The deceased was found on a train
How: Eaten by an animal
Who: A prominent media mogul with a dark family past
Detail: A witness has tampered with the murder scene

Murder Scene #122

Where: The victim was found in an airfield
How: Drug overdose
Who: An obnoxious journalist who held the key to a secret
Detail: Some photos are missing from the victim's briefcase

Murder Scene #123

Where: The victim was found on a factory floor
How: Poisoned water
Who: A timid sales promoter
Detail: The victim held a torn piece of paper in his hand

Murder Scene #124

Where: The deceased was found in a concert venue
How: Poisoned bandaid
Who: A wilful teenage pop idol
Detail: There was a strong smell of alcohol on the victim's body

Murder Scene #125

Where: The victim was found in a gas station stop
How: Poisoned ketchup
Who: A truck mechanic who was hiding something that happened two decades ago
Detail: A witness saw the victim exchanging something with someone in a car

Murder Scene #126

Where: The body was found in a gentleman's club
How: Fatal allergic reaction to seafood
Who: A sportswriter who is having an affair
Detail: A witness saw the victim running out of his home

Murder Scene #127

Where: The deceased was found hanging from a bridge
How: Stabbed in the back with a dagger
Who: A famous crime author whose books told too much
Detail: The murderer had left behind a clue on the victim's hair

Murder Scene #128

Where: The victim was found in a cloakroom
How: Skinned alive
Who: A fashionable socialite who recently came into an inheritance
Detail: The victim had suspected her husband of having an affair

Murder Scene #129

Where: The deceased was found in a resort
How: Throat cut by a broken mirror piece
Who: A home economics teacher
Detail: The victim received an odd message on her mobile phone before she died

Murder Scene #130

Where: The body was found in an animal shelter
How: Drowned to death in a barrel

Who: A heiress who was disfigured in a terrible accident years ago
Detail: The victim had left behind a note

Murder Scene #131

Where: The victim was found in a lift lobby
How: Burnt alive
Who: An novelist whose entire life was a lie
Detail: A burnt locket was found at the crime scene

Murder Scene #132

Where: The deceased was found in an opera box
How: Poisoned nail polish
Who: A theatre patroness involved in shady business
Detail: The victim held a broken fan in her hand

Murder Scene #133

Where: The victim was found in a car
How: Toxic hair dye
Who: A belligerent automobile mechanic
Detail: A witness noticed the victim behaving secretively the day before

Murder Scene #134

Where: The deceased was found in a farm
How: Gored by a cow
Who: A pessimistic academic
Detail: There is adhesive residue on the victim's fingertips

Murder Scene #135

Where: The body was found in a shop basement
How: Multiple stab wounds
Who: A shop worker about to go to the police
Detail: There is a odd smudge at the victim's neck

Murder Scene #136

Where: The victim was found in a chocolate shop
How: Poisoned chocolate
Who: An undercover journalist

Detail: The weather proves to be the murderer's downfall

Murder Scene #137

Where: The body was found hanging from a window
How: Mercury poisoning
Who: Son of a shipping tycoon who was an important court witness
Detail: Someone witnessed the victim beating up someone furiously

Murder Scene #138

Where: The victim was found in a mountain valley
How: Decapitated by a wire
Who: A military officer with a dark past
Detail: The victim's ankle has a thin red line on it

Murder Scene #139

Where: The deceased was found in a female student dormitory
How: Stabbed in the throat with a pocket knife
Who: An arrogant valedictorian with enemies
Detail: The victim's hand is tightly clutched together

Murder Scene #140

Where: The deceased was found in a hotel lounge
How: Poisoned cocktail
Who: A haughty soprano in the middle of a sex scandal
Detail: There is some sort of powder on the victim's shoes

Murder Scene #141

Where: The deceased was found in a hospital room
How: Stabbed in the chest with a knife
Who: A famed animal rights activist
Detail: There are red spots on the victim's neck

Murder Scene #142

Where: The deceased was found hidden inside a couch
How: Stabbed in the chest with an icepick
Who: A film editor who held the key to a secret
Detail: The victim's notebook pages are all torn out

Murder Scene #143

Where: The deceased was found in a recording studio
How: Poisoned cigarette
Who: A prolific record producer who likes to keep to himself
Detail: The victim's home was ransacked

Murder Scene #144

Where: The deceased was found in an alleyway
How: Attacked by an anaconda
Who: An young millionaire with something to hide
Detail: A witness had heard a strange noise

Murder Scene #145

Where: The victim was found hanging from a crane
How: Crushed by a slab of concrete
Who: A construction worker who was hiding something
Detail: A witness saw the victim chasing after someone

Murder Scene #146

Where: The victim was found in his office
How: Stabbed in the eye with a chopstick
Who: A quarrelsome academic
Detail: The room of the crime scene was unusually cold

Murder Scene #147

Where: The deceased was found in a bus
How: Carbon monoxide poisoning
Who: A school bus driver who lied about something
Detail: Something is missing from the victim's wallet

Murder Scene #148

Where: The deceased was found in a hostel washroom
How: Stabbed in the eye with a syringe
Who: A interior designer who was having a love affair
Detail: The victim received a mysterious voice recording before he died

Murder Scene #149

Where: The body was found in a church
How: Stabbed in the back with a dagger
Who: A hospital chaplain with a strange tattoo on his body
Detail: The blood splatters on the walls do not match up

Murder Scene #150

Where: The deceased was found inside a cargo crate on a plane
How: Suffocated to death from low oxygen levels
Who: A foreign service officer with a troubled past
Detail: The victim received a mysterious voice recording before he died

Murder Scene #151

Where: The body was found on a balcony
How: Beaten to death with a heavy lamp
Who: A suave administrative assistant
Detail: The victim's neck is mottled

Murder Scene #152

Where: The body was found in a student hostel
How: Poisoned beer
Who: A star athlete competing in an upcoming sports tournament
Detail: Something is missing from the victim's belongings

Murder Scene #153

Where: The body was found on his bed
How: Poisoned smoke
Who: A casino pit boss
Detail: The victim had unexplainable bite marks on his leg

Murder Scene #154

Where: The victim was found in a candy shop
How: Warfarin poisoning
Who: A shopkeeper who is not what he seemed to be
Detail: The victim made a strange remark before he died

Murder Scene #155

Where: The victim was found in a medical school
How: Strangled by a belt
Who: A brilliant medical student embroiled in a scandal over his research
Detail: There is a black stain on the victim's fingernail

Murder Scene #156

Where: The victim was found in the forest
How: Cocaine intoxication
Who: A glamorous film starlet with a perverse hobby
Detail: The victim had sent out a message to her friends before she died

Murder Scene #157

Where: The body was found in a milk truck
How: Poison on a drinking straw
Who: A milk delivery driver
Detail: The victim's wife receives a threatening message

Murder Scene #158

Where: The deceased was found in a septic tank
How: Strangled by a braid of hair
Who: A shy social psychologist
Detail: The victim's forearm has tiny needle marks

Murder Scene #159

Where: The body was found hidden in a suitcase
How: Broken neck from a great fall
Who: A residence counselor who betrayed her family
Detail: The victim had confided in her doctor recently

Murder Scene #160

Where: The victim was found in a classroom
How: Bitten by a green mamba
Who: A temperamental teaching assistant
Detail: The victim died in an unusual posture

Murder Scene #161

Where: The deceased was found in a park
How: Strangled by bare hands
Who: A brash operations manager
Detail: There were crushed and broken leaves all around the body

Murder Scene #162

Where: The victim was found in a photography studio
How: Camera flash triggered gunshot
Who: A celebrity photographer
Detail: A long line of snapped thread is found at the crime scene

Murder Scene #163

Where: The body was found in a train station terminal
How: Spontaneous combustion
Who: A quarrelsome rail yard engineer
Detail: There is a needle mark on the victim's neck

Murder Scene #164

Where: The deceased was found in a farm
How: Attacked by wolves
Who: An interpreter for the hearing impaired
Detail: The victim had left behind a curious message

Murder Scene #165

Where: The victim was found in an airport
How: Lead poisoning
Who: A criminal lawyer who betrayed her country
Detail: Someone had videotaped the murder

Murder Scene #166

Where: The body was found in a landfill
How: Strangled by rope
Who: A special education administrator with a dark family past
Detail: There is a torn hole in the victim's trousers

Murder Scene #167

Where: The victim was found in an all-boys boarding school
How: Poison on the pages of a book
Who: A highly esteemed military judge with a fetish
Detail: The victim's hand seemed to be pointing at something

Murder Scene #168

Where: The deceased was found in a broom closet
How: Burnt alive with kerosene
Who: A fast food cook who does something strange every morning
Detail: The soles of the victim's shoes, which are a few metres away, are muddy

Murder Scene #169

Where: The victim was found in the street
How: Struck on the head by falling bricks
Who: A child support services worker working on a case
Detail: Two reliable witnesses gave conflicting accounts of the same event

Murder Scene #170

Where: The victim was found in an all-girls boarding school
How: Suffocated to death with a pillow
Who: A popular student from a wealthy family
Detail: A burnt pantyhose was found near the crime scene

Murder Scene #171

Where: The body was found on the railway tracks in an underground tunnel
How: Throat slit by a razor blade
Who: An journalist who was having a love affair
Detail: The murderer had dropped a clue near the body in his haste

Murder Scene #172

Where: The deceased was found inside a fountain in a private mansion
How: Stabbed in the stomach with a samurai sword
Who: A vengeful business mogul
Detail: The victim had received something unusual in the mail before he

died

Murder Scene #173

Where: The victim was found in a wine cellar
How: Death from inhalation of a deadly gas
Who: A diplomat who was a corporate spy
Detail: A witness saw the victim exchanging something with someone in a car

Murder Scene #174

Where: The body was found in a lawyer's office
How: Stung to death by bees
Who: A lawyer who had seen something he shouldn't
Detail: There was a hastily written note stuffed in the victim's pocket

Murder Scene #175

Where: The deceased was found in a mortuary
How: Fatal allergic reaction to something in a corpse
Who: A temperamental mortuary assistant
Detail: A witness heard the victim boasting about something

Murder Scene #176

Where: The body was found in a hostel lounge
How: A gunshot wound in the head
Who: A well-liked student coordinator
Detail: There are strange marks on the victim's wrists

Murder Scene #177

Where: The victim was found on his bed
How: Gored by a cow
Who: A cocky conservation scientist
Detail: Someone received a call from the murderer after the victim was killed

Murder Scene #178

Where: The deceased was found on a hotel roof
How: Struck on the head with a cleaver

Who: An unpopular opera singer
Detail: A witness saw the victim chasing after someone

Murder Scene #179

Where: The body was found in a public library
How: Starvation
Who: A library assistant with an unusual habit
Detail: The murderer had an accomplice

Murder Scene #180

Where: The deceased was found on a hotel bed
How: Throttled to death with a bath towel
Who: A medical technologist who was on the run
Detail: The door of the crime scene was locked from the inside

Murder Scene #181

Where: The body was found at the bottom of a well
How: Stabbed in the eye with scissors
Who: An egoistical office clerk on holiday
Detail: There is a grey substance on the victim's thumb

Murder Scene #182

Where: The victim was found in an eatery
How: Bitten by a rattlesnake
Who: A combat engineer who was two-timing his girlfriend
Detail: A witness saw the victim running out of his home

Murder Scene #183

Where: The victim was found on a motorbike
How: Poisoned hair spray
Who: A golf course superintendent
Detail: The victim's water was drugged

Murder Scene #184

Where: The deceased was found in the lobby of an apartment building
How: Struck in the stomach with a crossbow arrow
Who: An insurance underwriter who was being threatened

Detail: Something is missing from the victim's belongings

Murder Scene #185

Where: The victim was found in the washroom of a train
How: Battered to death with a golf club
Who: A radio personality who is not what he seemed to be
Detail: A witness is lying

Murder Scene #186

Where: The victim was found at a pier
How: Strangled by rope
Who: A runaway teenager who had undergone plastic surgery
Detail: The victim's hand is frozen in an odd gesture

Murder Scene #187

Where: The victim was found inside a mailroom
How: Bitten by a snake inside a mailing envelope
Who: A post office worker
Detail: A witness has tampered with the murder scene

Murder Scene #188

Where: The body was found under the floorboards
How: Smothered to death with a cushion
Who: An outspoken survey researcher
Detail: A witness heard the murderer's voice

Murder Scene #189

Where: The body was found in a television studio
How: Throat slit by a blade
Who: A materialistic TV sports announcer about to reveal something to the press
Detail: A lock of hair was found at the crime scene

Murder Scene #190

Where: The victim was found in the toilet
How: Bitten by a black widow spider
Who: A taxi driver who stole something

Detail: The victim's car had been ransacked

Murder Scene #191

Where: The body was found in a slaughter house
How: Steamed to death
Who: An ambitious military analyst
Detail: A page is torn from the victim's diary

Murder Scene #192

Where: The body was found on the roof top of a train
How: A gunshot wound in the head
Who: A highly respected film editor with a secret
Detail: The victim's mobile phone was bugged

Murder Scene #193

Where: The deceased was found in a subway
How: Pushed into the path of an incoming train
Who: A pediatrician who found something suspicious
Detail: An envelope is missing from the victim's bag

Murder Scene #194

Where: The deceased was found in the living room
How: Poisoned fingernail
Who: A jealous psychiatrist
Detail: There is a shattered glass of water beside the body

Murder Scene #195

Where: The deceased was found in a golf course
How: Struck on the head by a boomerang
Who: A middle-aged professional golfer who was facing relationship problems
Detail: The body had been dragged for a distance

Murder Scene #196

Where: The body was found in a wine cellar
How: Stabbed in the head with a corkscrew
Who: A socialite who is not what she seemed to be

Detail: There was a note pinned to the victim's chest

Murder Scene #197

Where: The body was found in a public washroom
How: Throat cut by a broken mirror piece
Who: A proud special forces officer
Detail: The blood splatters on the walls do not match up

Murder Scene #198

Where: The victim was found in a rescue float in the sea
How: Bitten to death by a great white shark
Who: A payroll clerk about to expose her boss
Detail: There are marks around the victim's mouth

Murder Scene #199

Where: The victim was found by a lake
How: Poisoned flower pollen
Who: A prominent social work professor
Detail: The victim tore something up before he died

Murder Scene #200

Where: The body was found buried in quicksand
How: Struck on the head with a fire poker
Who: A entertainment agent
Detail: The victim had left behind a note

MURDER SCENES #201 - 300

Murder Scene #201

Where: The body was found in an all-boys boarding school
How: Fatal allergic reaction to oatmeal
Who: A school master
Detail: All the witnesses have something to hide

Murder Scene #202

Where: The deceased was found on a hostel bed
How: Death from malnutrition
Who: A teenage fashion model in a fatal romance with a deadly nutritionist
Detail: The victim had kept a diary

Murder Scene #203

Where: The deceased was found in a yacht
How: Dismembered alive by hatchet
Who: A ruthless drug kingpin
Detail: Some torn papers were found in the water near the crime scene

Murder Scene #204

Where: The victim was found in a drain
How: Strangled with underwear
Who: A missionary worker being blackmailed
Detail: A witness saw the victim running out of his home

Murder Scene #205

Where: The victim was found in a private swimming pool
How: Poisoned wine
Who: A demanding corporate CEO
Detail: There is something suspicious about a stain on the victim's leg

Murder Scene #206

Where: The victim was found in the washroom of a bar
How: Struck on the head by a brick
Who: A preschool teacher who suspected her husband of cheating on her
Detail: The victim died in an unusual posture

Murder Scene #207

Where: The victim was found in a television studio
How: Anthrax poisoning
Who: An outspoken women's rights activist pushing for a new bill
Detail: The victim held a torn photograph in her hand

Murder Scene #208

Where: The deceased was found in a field of wheat
How: Struck on the head by a spade
Who: A wildlife biologist who does something strange every day
Detail: A thumb drive is missing from the victim's handbag

Murder Scene #209

Where: The deceased was found in a refuse dump
How: A gunshot wound in the chest
Who: A prestigious horticulturist who was going to unveil his research findings
Detail: A plant specimen is missing from the victim's workplace

Murder Scene #210

Where: The victim was found in his study room
How: Throat slit by a razor blade
Who: A judge who was harbouring a criminal
Detail: The victim's fingernails have an unidentified substance underneath them

Murder Scene #211

Where: The deceased was found in a crate in the woods
How: Poisoned cutlery
Who: A famed cafeteria cook about to break into the national limelight
Detail: The victim had left behind a coded message in a recipe

Murder Scene #212

Where: The victim was found in a septic tank
How: Boiled to death
Who: A quick-tempered administrative assistant

Detail: A secret cipher is involved

Murder Scene #213

Where: The deceased was found on a swing
How: Fatal allergic reaction to a wasp sting
Who: A young heiress involved in a family feud
Detail: The prime suspect has a solid alibi

Murder Scene #214

Where: The victim was found at the bottom of a river
How: Stabbed in the back with an icepick
Who: A brilliant TV personality
Detail: The victim had received something unusual in the mail before he died

Murder Scene #215

Where: The victim was found in a forest
How: Struck on the head with a heavy walking cane
Who: A TV personality who was a victim of domestic abuse some years ago
Detail: A witness noticed the victim in tears the day before

Murder Scene #216

Where: The body was found in a chimney
How: Strangled by an electrical cord
Who: A middle school teacher with a dark family secret
Detail: The victim's shoes are missing

Murder Scene #217

Where: The victim was found encased in a wall
How: Dismembered alive by chainsaw
Who: A middle school vocational education teacher
Detail: The victim's clothes are oily with something

Murder Scene #218

Where: The victim was found in a swamp
How: Stabbed in the eye with a scalpel

Who: A highly respected geography professor
Detail: There was a map in the victim's pocket

Murder Scene #219

Where: The body was found in a female student dormitory
How: Suffocation to death with plaster around the head
Who: A popular student involved in a love triangle
Detail: There was no sign of a struggle

Murder Scene #220

Where: The victim was found in a restaurant kitchen
How: Throat sliced with a thin wire
Who: A TV sports announcer who was having work problems
Detail: Someone witnessed the victim destroying a tape recording

Murder Scene #221

Where: The deceased was found at the foot of an apartment building
How: Fell to death from a great height
Who: A music composer
Detail: A clue to the murderer may be in the composer's music lyrics

Murder Scene #222

Where: The deceased was found on his bed
How: Burnt to death with a blow torch
Who: A corrupt marine surveyor
Detail: There are red scratches on the victim's desk

Murder Scene #223

Where: The victim was found under a tree
How: A gunshot wound in the head
Who: A well-respected military policeman who was acquitted from a crime some years ago
Detail: There was something in the victim's pocket

Murder Scene #224

Where: The body was found in a school stairwell
How: Struck on the head by a heavy vase

Who: A university professor covering up for somebody
Detail: There is a odd smudge at the victim's neck

Murder Scene #225

Where: The body was found in an art musuem
How: Toxic paint on an artwork
Who: A strict musuem curator
Detail: The victim's car had been ransacked

Murder Scene #226

Where: The victim was found on a cruise ship
How: Stabbed in the chest with a knife
Who: A seaman who was being threatened
Detail: A witness heard the murderer's voice

Murder Scene #227

Where: The deceased was found on a balcony
How: Stabbed in the eye with a fork
Who: A widow with links to the mafia
Detail: There is a strong scent in the crime scene

Murder Scene #228

Where: The victim was found in a camping site
How: Suffocation to death with a pillow
Who: An animal scientist who was facing relationship problems
Detail: A broken bit of plastic is found near the crime scene

Murder Scene #229

Where: The deceased was found in a retail store
How: Broken neck by a falling TV set
Who: A likeable delivery driver
Detail: The victim's hand seemed to be pointing at something

Murder Scene #230

Where: The body was found in his study room
How: Injection with poison from a pen
Who: An elderly business tycoon in the midst of deciding his will

Detail: A family member noticed the victim in distress the day before

Murder Scene #231

Where: The body was found in a clothing shop
How: Toxic socks
Who: An obnoxious psychiatric aide
Detail: The victim's hand is tightly clutched around an object

Murder Scene #232

Where: The deceased was found inside a disused fridge in a refuse yard
How: Suffocation to death
Who: A beautiful insurance lawyer
Detail: The murder took place in the heat of summer

Murder Scene #233

Where: The victim was found on a soccer pitch
How: Killed by a soccer ball
Who: A famous soccer player who is having multiple love affairs
Detail: The murderer had an accomplice

Murder Scene #234

Where: The deceased was found in the backseat of a luxury car
How: Stabbed in the head with a corkscrew
Who: A rock star who was an ex-convict
Detail: The lock to the victim's home was broken

Murder Scene #235

Where: The victim was found in a bar
How: Skinned alive
Who: A bar owner
Detail: The victim had suspected his wife of having an affair

Murder Scene #236

Where: The deceased was found backstage
How: Struck on the head with a guitar
Who: A charismatic girl band pop idol whose entire life was a lie
Detail: There is a blue stain on the victim's coat

Murder Scene #237

Where: The body was found on a swing
How: Beheaded with a cleaver
Who: A glamorous model who was an undercover agent
Detail: The blood splatters on the ground do not match up

Murder Scene #238

Where: The body was found in a park
How: Knife stab in the stomach
Who: A biological technician in possession of lab secrets
Detail: A witness saw the victim speaking with someone in a car

Murder Scene #239

Where: The body was found in the forest
How: Bitten by a ferocious animal
Who: A demanding highway patrolman
Detail: The victim's ankle has a thin red line on it

Murder Scene #240

Where: The deceased was found in a lake
How: Death from inhalation of deadly chloramine gas
Who: A conceited marine architect with a penchant for beautiful women
Detail: The victim's wrist watch stopped at midnight

Murder Scene #241

Where: The body was found in a canal
How: Fatal sting from scorpion
Who: A well-respected field health officer who lied to his wife
Detail: The victim was suffering from a nose bleed

Murder Scene #242

Where: The deceased was found in a shed
How: Attacked by a crocodile
Who: A medical secretary with a mysterious family background
Detail: There was something smeared on the victim's forehead

Murder Scene #243

Where: The body was found on a hotel roof
How: Struck on the throat with a cleaver
Who: A materialistic truck driver transporting something illegal
Detail: A broken crate was found near the crime scene

Murder Scene #244

Where: The body was found in a retail store after closing hours
How: Multiple slash wounds
Who: An obnoxious retail supervisor
Detail: A witness saw the victim having an intense conversation with someone

Murder Scene #245

Where: The body was found in a lighthouse
How: Lethal injection of poison
Who: A lighthouse keeper
Detail: The victim had sent out a message to his friends before he died

Murder Scene #246

Where: The body was found in a male student dormitory
How: Strangled by pantyhose
Who: A star athlete student
Detail: A twisted ring was found at the crime scene

Murder Scene #247

Where: The victim was found propped against the door
How: Strangled by a ribbon
Who: A medical secretary who visits somewhere odd every evening
Detail: There was a red thread tied around the victim's wrist

Murder Scene #248

Where: The victim was found in a church
How: Carbon monoxide poisoning
Who: A controversial exhibit artist
Detail: Someone saw the victim in an unexpected place before he died

Murder Scene #249

Where: The victim was found inside a block of cement
How: Stabbed in the eye with a syringe
Who: A quarrelsome special forces officer
Detail: The victim had complained of someone stalking him

Murder Scene #250

Where: The deceased was found in a cage
How: Attacked by a pet ape
Who: An advertising executive with a dark past
Detail: All the witnesses have something to hide

Murder Scene #251

Where: The victim was found inside a gym
How: Throttled to death by a gym machine
Who: A fitness trainer who was having a love affair with a client
Detail: A witness has heard the murderer's voice

Murder Scene #252

Where: The victim was found under a bridge
How: Polonium poisoning
Who: An sales engineer with bizarre markings on his body
Detail: The victim's clothes are missing

Murder Scene #253

Where: The deceased was found on a ship mast
How: Hung to death from a noose
Who: A bossy commercial fisherman
Detail: There is a grey substance on the victim's thumb

Murder Scene #254

Where: The body was found on a car racing track
How: Ricin poisoning
Who: An opinionated computer security specialist
Detail: The murderer had an accomplice

Murder Scene #255

Where: The body was found in the driver's seat of a car
How: Bitten by a puff adder
Who: A TV sports announcer with a penchant for vintage cars
Detail: There was a smear of ink on the victim's hand

Murder Scene #256

Where: The body was found in a timber mill
How: Drowned in a barrel
Who: A social service volunteer embroiled in a scandal
Detail: A witness noticed the victim in tears the day before

Murder Scene #257

Where: The deceased was found at the foot of an apartment building
How: Struck on the head by a falling vase
Who: A strict kindergarten teacher
Detail: A witness had heard a strange noise

Murder Scene #258

Where: The body was found in a garden nursery
How: Drowning
Who: A mental health counselor who was visiting a patient
Detail: A lipstick mark was found on the victim's shirt

Murder Scene #259

Where: The deceased was found in a video rental shop
How: Lethal injection of poison
Who: A correction officer with a dark past
Detail: The victim brushed past someone suspicious before he died

Murder Scene #260

Where: The deceased was found on a horse stable
How: Kicked to death by a horse
Who: A well regarded financial planner
Detail: There is a strong smell at the crime scene

Murder Scene #261

Where: The victim was found in at the foot of an apartment block
How: Fell to his death from his apartment home
Who: A domineering police officer who was having work problems
Detail: A long line of snapped thread is found at the crime scene

Murder Scene #262

Where: The deceased was found in a shack
How: Stabbed in the eye with a steak knife
Who: A bossy educational administrator who was hiding something that happened a decade ago
Detail: Someone had videotaped the murder

Murder Scene #263

Where: The victim was found in an animal shelter
How: Strangled to death with a leash
Who: A homeless woman who saw something she shouldn't
Detail: A witness had heard a strange noise

Murder Scene #264

Where: The deceased was found in a movie theatre
How: Poisoned dart from a blow gun
Who: A famous actor with a jealous rival
Detail: There is an unidentified powder on the victim's wrist

Murder Scene #265

Where: The body was found in a caravan van
How: Beheaded with an axe
Who: A teenage boy
Detail: A witness saw the victim speaking to someone in a car

Murder Scene #266

Where: The deceased was found hanging from a window
How: Thallium sulfate poisoning
Who: A sexy psychiatrist who held the key to a secret
Detail: The victim's watch is missing

Murder Scene #267

Where: The body was found in a slaughter house
How: Trampled to death by pigs
Who: A perfectionist high school teacher
Detail: The victim's hair is sticky with something

Murder Scene #268

Where: The deceased was found in a river
How: Throat slit by a razor blade
Who: A community organization worker who is not what she seemed to be
Detail: The victim died in an unusual posture

Murder Scene #269

Where: The body was found in the toilet
How: Mercury poisoning
Who: An animal scientist facing a divorce
Detail: There is a rip in the victim's pants

Murder Scene #270

Where: The victim was found in a garbage bin
How: Decapitated by a wire
Who: A gifted writer
Detail: The victim had left a strange message on his phone the day he died

Murder Scene #271

Where: The body was found in an ice box
How: Struck on the head by a heavy ashtray
Who: An overworked social worker
Detail: The victim had suspected her husband of having an affair

Murder Scene #272

Where: The deceased was found in a field of wheat
How: Shot in the head by a nailgun
Who: A biomedical engineer who was blackmailing somebody
Detail: There was no sign of a struggle

Murder Scene #273

Where: The body was found in a park
How: Hypothermia
Who: An abusive celebrity photographer with a troubled past
Detail: The victim's shoes are missing

Murder Scene #274

Where: The body was found hanging from a window
How: Fatal allergic reaction to hay
Who: A sales engineer who had seen something he shouldn't
Detail: There are scratches on the victim's hands

Murder Scene #275

Where: The victim was found in a hotel room
How: Head struck by a heavy lamp
Who: A provocative TV star
Detail: The murderer had left behind a clue on the victim's lips

Murder Scene #276

Where: The body was found inside a fountain
How: Electrocution
Who: A fashion designer who plagiarized designs
Detail: Someone received a call from the murderer after the victim was killed

Murder Scene #277

Where: The body was found in a restaurant
How: Poisoned pasta
Who: A controlling cardiologist
Detail: There was something strange about the way the victim held the cutlery

Murder Scene #278

Where: The deceased was found in the bathtub
How: Struck on the head with an icepick
Who: A glamorous TV personality
Detail: The victim's hair is dry

Murder Scene #279

Where: The body was found in the wheel well of an airplane
How: A gunshot wound in the chest
Who: An argumentative aircraft mechanic who was an ex-CIA agent
Detail: There is a black mark on the victim's fingernail

Murder Scene #280

Where: The deceased was found in a motorbike crash
How: Poisoned beer
Who: A veterinarian
Detail: The victim had complained of someone stalking him

Murder Scene #281

Where: The body was found in a drain
How: Struck on the throat with a cleaver
Who: A well-known restaurant owner
Detail: The victim has a red line on her forehead

Murder Scene #282

Where: The victim was found at the seashore
How: Beaten to death with a fence plank
Who: A brash zoologist
Detail: A charcoal mark was found on the victim's shirt

Murder Scene #283

Where: The body was found in an art musuem
How: Stabbed in the throat with a pocket knife
Who: A tax lawyer with money issues
Detail: The murder took place after closing hours

Murder Scene #284

Where: The body was found in a train station terminal
How: Pushed into the path of an incoming train
Who: A well-respected airline pilot
Detail: Something is missing from the victim's wallet

Murder Scene #285

Where: The victim was found in her home
How: Strangled by curtains
Who: A bossy community organization worker
Detail: A glove is missing from the victim's hand

Murder Scene #286

Where: The body was found in the shower
How: Stabbed in the back with a knife
Who: An aloof actress who was disfigured in a terrible accident years ago
Detail: The blood splatters on the walls do not match up

Murder Scene #287

Where: The deceased was found buried in the woods
How: Run over by a car
Who: A foreign language interpreter in heavy debt
Detail: Someone saw the victim in an unexpected place before he died

Murder Scene #288

Where: The victim was found tied in the backseat of a car
How: Carbon monoxide poisoning
Who: A student admissions administrator who takes bribes
Detail: A witness heard the victim bragging about something

Murder Scene #289

Where: The deceased was found in an alley
How: Strangled by bare hands
Who: An abusive TV personality who suspected her boyfriend of cheating on her
Detail: A witness had seen the victim behaving strangely the day she died

Murder Scene #290

Where: The body was found in a corridor
How: Struck in the stomach with an axe
Who: A paranoid heiress
Detail: The victim's niece received something in the mail from the victim before she died

Murder Scene #291

Where: The body was found under a bridge
How: Struck on the head by a falling brick
Who: An ambitious radio talk show host who lied about her past
Detail: The body had been dragged for a distance

Murder Scene #292

Where: The victim was found in an underground tunnel
How: Burnt to death with kerosene
Who: A prominent chief financial officer who was an important court witness
Detail: The victim's wrist watch stopped at midnight

Murder Scene #293

Where: The body was found on his bed
How: Throat cut by a broken mirror piece
Who: A detective in the middle of a difficult case
Detail: A stash of strange photos was found in the victim's home

Murder Scene #294

Where: The deceased was found in a greenhouse
How: Stung to death by fire ants
Who: A quick-tempered socialite
Detail: The victim's belt is missing

Murder Scene #295

Where: The body was found in a landfill
How: Dismembered alive by chainsaw
Who: A truck mechanic who was having work problems
Detail: A body part is missing

Murder Scene #296

Where: The deceased was found in a construction site
How: Broken neck from a falling sack of concrete
Who: A frustrated crime journalist
Detail: The victim's shirt pocket had been ripped off

Murder Scene #297

Where: The victim was found in a garden
How: Electrocution
Who: An elderly football star who was involved in a scandal decades ago
Detail: The victim received an odd message on his mobile phone before his died

Murder Scene #298

Where: The body was found in an abandoned boat by the river
How: Multiple gunshot wounds
Who: An economics professor
Detail: A missing key to a safe is involved

Murder Scene #299

Where: The body was found in a public library
How: Poisoned water
Who: A speech pathologist who does something strange every morning
Detail: The victim was gagged

Murder Scene #300

Where: The body was found in the boot of a car
How: Carbon monoxide poisoning
Who: A marketing manager about to expose her boss
Detail: A witness heard the victim boasting about something

MURDER SCENES #301 - 400

Murder Scene #301

Where: The body was found in a dumpster
How: Crushed in a waste compactor
Who: A prominent basketball star who is an alcoholic
Detail: There were crushed glass pieces all around the body

Murder Scene #302

Where: The victim was found in a grandstand
How: Stabbed in the stomach with a knife
Who: A sportswriter
Detail: There is a cufflink missing from the victim's clothes

Murder Scene #303

Where: The body was found in a bakery
How: Attacked by an anaconda
Who: A young management consultant
Detail: A witness is concealing important evidence

Murder Scene #304

Where: The victim was found in a fast food outlet
How: Struck on the head with a hammer
Who: A university professor with a troubled past
Detail: Something is abnormal about the victim's hand

Murder Scene #305

Where: The victim was found on a balcony
How: Dehydration
Who: A brilliant mining engineer
Detail: All the witnesses have something to hide

Murder Scene #306

Where: The victim was found in a sports stadium
How: Hung to death from a noose
Who: A flight engineer who had undergone plastic surgery
Detail: There was no sign of a struggle

Murder Scene #307

Where: The deceased was found in a canal
How: Bludgeoned to death with a crowbar
Who: A wanted fugitive
Detail: The victim held a torn ticket in his hand

Murder Scene #308

Where: The victim was found in a military bunker
How: Dismembered alive by axe
Who: A pessimistic missionary worker
Detail: A torn jacket is found near the crime scene

Murder Scene #309

Where: The body was found in a hotel toilet
How: Strangled by computer cables
Who: A temperamental fraud investigator
Detail: The victim was drugged

Murder Scene #310

Where: The victim was found in a cable car
How: Stabbed in the neck with a knife
Who: A well-liked hospital chaplain
Detail: The blood splatters on the walls do not match up

Murder Scene #311

Where: The deceased was found in a press room
How: Strangled by a belt
Who: An alcoholic ship pilot
Detail: The victim's wrist band is missing

Murder Scene #312

Where: The body was found at the bottom of a river
How: Drowned
Who: A shipping clerk who was an undercover journalist
Detail: Secret documents was found in the victim's laptop

Murder Scene #313

Where: The deceased was found tied to a horse
How: Poisoned water
Who: A compulsive restaurant owner
Detail: The victim had suspected his wife of having an affair

Murder Scene #314

Where: The victim was found in a shop basement
How: Bitten by a black mamba
Who: A wildlife biologist who had an affair with her boss
Detail: The victim had strange bruises on his foot

Murder Scene #315

Where: The deceased was found inside a dumpster
How: Multiple slash wounds
Who: An espionage intelligence agent
Detail: A burnt dog collar was found near the crime scene

Murder Scene #316

Where: The deceased was found in the bedroom
How: Struck on the head by a heavy ashtray
Who: An loan interviewer with a family secret
Detail: The victim's mobile phone was bugged

Murder Scene #317

Where: The victim was found in the basement of a house
How: Strangled by bedsheets
Who: A cocky superstar
Detail: There are red scratches on the victim's face

Murder Scene #318

Where: The body was found in a movie theatre
How: Spontaneous combustion
Who: A corrupt insurance lawyer
Detail: There was a strong smell of alcohol on the victim's body

Murder Scene #319

Where: The victim was found in the backseat of a luxury car
How: Strangled by a wig
Who: A parole officer who was having a love affair with a student
Detail: The murderer had an accomplice

Murder Scene #320

Where: The victim was found in a timber mill
How: Gunshot wound to the chest
Who: A scientist cheating on his wife
Detail: A witness is lying

Murder Scene #321

Where: The body was found in a dormitory washroom
How: Poisoned hair spray
Who: A frustrated high school student with a jealous rival
Detail: There is something odd about the victim's wardrobe

Murder Scene #322

Where: The deceased was found on a factory floor
How: Fell to death from a high floor
Who: A wanted fugitive who discovered a secret
Detail: There is an oily residue on the victim's fingertips

Murder Scene #323

Where: The victim was found in bed
How: Toxic underwear
Who: A copy writer who was planning to resign
Detail: The victim had sent out a message to her friends before she died

Murder Scene #324

Where: The deceased was found on a basketball court
How: Stabbed in the eye with a pocket knife
Who: A quick-tempered school teacher who likes to keep to herself
Detail: A broken watch was found at the crime scene

Murder Scene #325

Where: The deceased was found inside a musuem
How: Crushed by a falling monument
Who: A finance manager blackmailing someone
Detail: Someone received a call from the murderer after the victim was killed

Murder Scene #326

Where: The victim was found by a lake
How: Carbon monoxide poisoning
Who: A hotel lobby attendant who saw something he shouldn't
Detail: A black smear on the victim's arm may provide a clue to the murderer's identity

Murder Scene #327

Where: The victim was found in an abandoned factory
How: Buried alive in concrete
Who: A bad-tempered advertising account executive
Detail: Someone had videotaped the murder

Murder Scene #328

Where: The body was found in a retail store
How: A gunshot wound in the head
Who: A policeman who was involved in a domestic abuse case some years ago
Detail: The murderer had dropped a clue near the body in her haste

Murder Scene #329

Where: The victim was found in the backseat of a luxury car
How: Stung to death by wasps
Who: A clergy member
Detail: Something is missing from the victim's desk

Murder Scene #330

Where: The body was found hanging from a crane
How: Toxic makeup
Who: A call girl

Detail: There are strange marks on the victim's eyelids

Murder Scene #331

Where: The victim was found in the sea in an overturned bus
How: Drowned
Who: A callous bus driver
Detail: The victim had unexplainable markings on his forearm

Murder Scene #332

Where: The victim was found in an observatory science centre
How: Electrocuted
Who: A quarrelsome inventor
Detail: The victim's hand was tied behind his back

Murder Scene #333

Where: The body was found in a refuse dump
How: Beheaded with a wire
Who: An obnoxious pop singer who does something strange every day
Detail: There were bits of glass around the body

Murder Scene #334

Where: The body was found in a chimney
How: Run over by a car
Who: A financial analyst who was two-timing her boyfriend
Detail: There are red scars on the victim's neck

Murder Scene #335

Where: The victim was found in a luxury home
How: Bitten by a yellow sac spider
Who: A music director with a gambling problem
Detail: The lock to the victim's home was broken

Murder Scene #336

Where: The body was found in the waters of a fish farm
How: Struck on the head by a heavy object
Who: A renowned tycoon
Detail: The victim's shirt buttons were ripped off

Murder Scene #337

Where: The deceased was found in a caravan van
How: Choked to death on soap
Who: An elementary school teacher
Detail: Someone witnessed the victim berating someone furiously

Murder Scene #338

Where: The victim was found in a mountain valley
How: Poisoned by antifreeze
Who: A highly respected investor
Detail: The lock to the victim's home was broken

Murder Scene #339

Where: The victim was found in a printing house
How: Poisoned fumes
Who: A well regarded editor
Detail: There was a letter in the victim's pocket

Murder Scene #340

Where: The deceased was found in a walk-in freezer
How: Dismembered alive by machete
Who: A farm hand with family trouble
Detail: A witness noticed the victim in tears the day before

Murder Scene #341

Where: The victim was found in a church pew
How: Poison on a drinking straw
Who: A retired sailor who keeps to himself
Detail: A thumb drive is missing from the victim's pocket

Murder Scene #342

Where: The body was found on the railway tracks in an underground tunnel
How: Attacked by an anaconda
Who: A drug dealer who betrayed his country
Detail: A witness noticed the victim in a panic the day before

Murder Scene #343

Where: The body was found hidden inside a bale of straw
How: Stabbed in the eye with a corkscrew
Who: A family practitioner facing a lawsuit
Detail: The victim made a strange remark before he died

Murder Scene #344

Where: The victim was found on a hiking trail
How: Warfarin poisoning
Who: A mechanical engineer who was being laid off
Detail: The victim was blindfolded

Murder Scene #345

Where: The body was found underwater in a tourist attraction
How: Bitten by an animal
Who: A quarrelsome music professor
Detail: The victim's shoelace is missing

Murder Scene #346

Where: The body was found in a boat
How: Poisoned hair comb
Who: An egoistical police officer
Detail: A frayed rope is found at the crime scene

Murder Scene #347

Where: The deceased was found at the harbour
How: Multiple injuries in head from hammered in nails
Who: A social service volunteer
Detail: A secret cipher is involved

Murder Scene #348

Where: The body was found in an alley
How: Stabbed in the chest with an icepick
Who: A math professor
Detail: There was a strong smell of perfume at the crime scene

Murder Scene #349

Where: The victim was found in a washroom
How: Poisoned toilet paper
Who: A perfectionist restaurant manager
Detail: A witness saw the murderer's hand

Murder Scene #350

Where: The victim was found in a shack
How: Struck on the head with a crowbar
Who: An upcoming fashion model
Detail: The victim had left behind a note

Murder Scene #351

Where: The deceased was found under the floorboards
How: Head struck by a TV set
Who: A wealthy venture capitalist
Detail: There is something suspicious about a stain on the victim's leg

Murder Scene #352

Where: The body was found in a garbage bin
How: Toxic clothing
Who: An Oscar winning actress
Detail: The victim had suspected her husband of having an affair

Murder Scene #353

Where: The victim was found in a stairwell
How: Clobbered to death with a rolling pin
Who: A child support investigator
Detail: The victim's ankle has a thin red line on it

Murder Scene #354

Where: The victim was found in the toilet
How: Stabbed in the eye with an icepick
Who: A beautiful author who was two-timing her boyfriend
Detail: A witness heard the victim complaining about something

Murder Scene #355

Where: The body was found on the bonnet of a car
How: Throat slit by broken glass
Who: A middle-aged executive who was a corporate spy
Detail: The victim's notebook pages are all torn out

Murder Scene #356

Where: The victim was found in a resort
How: Stabbed in the stomach with a dagger
Who: A famed pianist
Detail: The victim's fingers were chopped off

Murder Scene #357

Where: The victim was found by a lamp post
How: Poisoned tea
Who: A patent lawyer who likes to brag
Detail: The victim's mobile phone was bugged

Murder Scene #358

Where: The deceased was found in a camping site
How: Poisoned toilet paper
Who: A brilliant biologist
Detail: The victim was gagged

Murder Scene #359

Where: The deceased was found in a car factory
How: Stabbed in the stomach with a knife
Who: A mafia gang leader who was blackmailing somebody
Detail: The victim's hand is tightly clutched around a pole

Murder Scene #360

Where: The deceased was found in a dentist's chair
How: Multiple injuries in head from a dentist drill
Who: An unpopular correspondence clerk who likes to keep to himself
Detail: The victim had sent out a coded message to his colleagues before he died

Murder Scene #361

Where: The victim was found by the cemetery gates
How: Cocaine intoxication
Who: A theatre patroness with a family secret
Detail: The victim had left behind a curious message

Murder Scene #362

Where: The victim was found in a shack
How: Poisoned cake
Who: A pop singer who was being threatened
Detail: The victim was wearing shoes that do not belong to her

Murder Scene #363

Where: The deceased was found in a theatre dressing room
How: Bitten by a black widow spider
Who: An actress who was having a love affair
Detail: There is something in the victim's mouth

Murder Scene #364

Where: The deceased was found in a cable car
How: Lethal injection of poison
Who: An authoritarian tax lawyer who lied about her past
Detail: There is a black stain on the victim's fingernail

Murder Scene #365

Where: The body was found in a concert venue
How: Throat cut by a razor blade
Who: A veterinary assistant
Detail: The body had been dragged for a distance

Murder Scene #366

Where: The deceased was found off a desolated road
How: Skinned alive
Who: A construction labourer who likes to keep to himself
Detail: A witness saw the murderer's masked face

Murder Scene #367

Where: The deceased was found in an ice box
How: Poisoned toothbrush
Who: A materialistic fashion artist
Detail: The victim's hair is wet

Murder Scene #368

Where: The victim was found in the living room
How: Poisoned smoke
Who: A widower with designs on his parents-in-laws' wealth
Detail: There is something in the victim's mouth

Murder Scene #369

Where: The deceased was found in a tar pit
How: Starvation
Who: A real estate broker who is not what he seemed to be
Detail: The victim's hands were tied together with vines

Murder Scene #370

Where: The body was found in a mud pit
How: Signs of being buried alive
Who: A deceptive administrative law judge
Detail: The victim has a bruise on his shoulder

Murder Scene #371

Where: The victim was found in a horse stable
How: Strychnine poisoning
Who: A film starlet who was hiding something
Detail: There are clay marks on the victim's heels

Murder Scene #372

Where: The deceased was found by a lake
How: Poisoned wine
Who: A teaching assistant with a gambling problem
Detail: There was a twist of red paper in the victim's hand

Murder Scene #373

Where: The victim was found in a television studio
How: Stabbed in the eye with a pair of scissors
Who: A promising actor who was about to be promoted
Detail: A witness has tampered with the murder scene

Murder Scene #374

Where: The body was found inside a community kitchen
How: Struck on the head with a heavy wooden cutting board
Who: A patent lawyer who betrayed her client
Detail: Someone witnessed the victim destroying a tape recording

Murder Scene #375

Where: The deceased was found in a chest
How: Toxic clothing
Who: A special education teacher
Detail: An inheritance will is involved

Murder Scene #376

Where: The deceased was found inside a clinic
How: Poisoned by antifreeze
Who: A special forces officer who was having a love affair
Detail: A glove is missing from the victim's hand

Murder Scene #377

Where: The body was found at the bottom of a cliff
How: Stabbed in the throat with a pocket knife
Who: A perfectionist TV producer
Detail: A witness saw the victim running out of his home

Murder Scene #378

Where: The deceased was found in a bar
How: Poisoned cocktail glass
Who: A proud stockbroker
Detail: Someone witnessed the victim berating someone furiously

Murder Scene #379

Where: The deceased was found in a canal
How: Struck on the head with an icepick
Who: An undercover journalist
Detail: There was a map in the victim's pocket

Murder Scene #380

Where: The victim was found in an eatery
How: Poisoned mayonnaise
Who: A immigration inspector who owes money
Detail: The victim had received something unusual in the mail before he
died

Murder Scene #381

Where: The victim was found at his office desk
How: Struck on the head with an axe
Who: An elderly psychology professor with enemies
Detail: The victim was trying to reach something

Murder Scene #382

Where: The deceased was found in an observatory science centre
How: Massive blood loss caused by slitting of wrist
Who: An intelligence specialist who betrayed her country
Detail: The victim had strange bruises on her arm

Murder Scene #383

Where: The body was found in a field of corn
How: Stabbed in the eye with a knitting needle
Who: An egoistical engineering manager
Detail: There are red scratches on the victim's face

Murder Scene #384

Where: The victim was found on the railway tracks in an underground
tunnel
How: Multiple stab wounds
Who: A taxi driver
Detail: A paw print was found near the body

Murder Scene #385

Where: The deceased was found in a candy shop
How: Poisoned candy wrapper
Who: A farmer with a family secret
Detail: There is an odd smudge at the victim's neck

Murder Scene #386

Where: The body was found in the boot of an abandoned car
How: Beaten to death
Who: A drug abuse counseller who was an ex-convict
Detail: The victim was bound and gagged

Murder Scene #387

Where: The deceased was found on the train tracks
How: Pushed into the path of an incoming train
Who: A gangster who lost all his money
Detail: There is an oily residue on the victim's fingertips

Murder Scene #388

Where: The body was found on a tennis court
How: Strangled to death with a shoelace
Who: A heiress who suspected her husband of cheating on her
Detail: The victim was drugged

Murder Scene #389

Where: The body was found in her hostel bed
How: Drowning
Who: A star student with an unusual tattoo on her body
Detail: The bed was wet, but the floor was completely dry

Murder Scene #390

Where: The deceased was found in a yacht
How: Poisoned dart from a blow gun
Who: A wealthy playboy
Detail: The victim's belt is missing

Murder Scene #391

Where: The body was found in a golf course
How: Lethal injection of poison
Who: A criminal investigator
Detail: There are deep scratches on the victim's desk

Murder Scene #392

Where: The body was found in a landfill
How: Burnt to death with a blow torch
Who: A medical assistant embroiled in a corporate scandal
Detail: The murderer had dropped a clue near the body in his haste

Murder Scene #393

Where: The victim was found in a lake
How: A fatal blow to the head
Who: A commercial airline pilot who lost a lot of money
Detail: A witness saw the victim shouting at someone

Murder Scene #394

Where: The body was found in a casino
How: Poisoned playing card
Who: A casino manager who held the key to a secret
Detail: Something is abnormal about the victim's fingers

Murder Scene #395

Where: The deceased was found under a bridge
How: Bludgeoned to death with a crowbar
Who: A ballistics expert
Detail: There is a deep cut on the victim's lips

Murder Scene #396

Where: The deceased was found inside a tour bus
How: Stabbed in the eye with a fork
Who: A bus driver who was leading a double life
Detail: The lock to the victim's home was broken

Murder Scene #397

Where: The body was found on a hiking trail
How: Struck on the head by a boomerang
Who: A dispatcher who was disfigured in a terrible accident years ago
Detail: The victim had received something unusual in the mail before he died

Murder Scene #398

Where: The deceased was found by a garden path
How: Bitten by a rattlesnake
Who: A rich industrialist going through a divorce
Detail: There is something suspicious about a stain on the victim's leg

Murder Scene #399

Where: The deceased was found in a hotel lounge
How: Poison on the screen of a mobile phone
Who: A prominent catwalk model
Detail: A secret cipher is involved

Murder Scene #400

Where: The deceased was found in a drain
How: Clobbered to death with a tree branch
Who: A camp director who was involved in a domestic abuse case some years ago
Detail: Someone witnessed the victim beating up someone furiously

MURDER SCENES #401 - 500

Murder Scene #401

Where: The body was found in a resort
How: Strangled by pantyhose
Who: A middle school teacher
Detail: A page is torn from the victim's diary

Murder Scene #402

Where: The body was found in a fast food outlet
How: Lye poisoning
Who: A record producer with marriage problems
Detail: The victim brushed past someone suspicious before he died

Murder Scene #403

Where: The body was found in an alleyway
How: Stabbed in the eye with a pen
Who: A town clerk with a fatal love
Detail: The victim's hair is wet

Murder Scene #404

Where: The victim was found inside a washroom
How: Strangled by a dog leash
Who: An ambitious politician
Detail: The victim held a torn bit of cloth in his hand

Murder Scene #405

Where: The body was found in a funeral parlor
How: Strangled by rope
Who: Daughter of a wealthy philanthropist
Detail: The victim had left a strange message on his phone the day she died

Murder Scene #406

Where: The deceased was found in a warehouse
How: Bitten to death by wild dogs
Who: An inventor who was facing patent problems
Detail: The victim's neck is mottled

Murder Scene #407

Where: The victim was found in a pub
How: Poison on a beer mug
Who: A promising professional boxer
Detail: Something is missing from the victim's belongings

Murder Scene #408

Where: The body was found in an all-boys boarding school
How: Fatal allergic reaction to perfume
Who: A popular teacher with a dark family past
Detail: The soles of the victim's shoes are muddy

Murder Scene #409

Where: The deceased was found in a wall
How: Death from suffocation
Who: A security guard who is not what she seemed to be
Detail: The victim's uniform has an odd stain on it

Murder Scene #410

Where: The victim was found in a shed
How: Struck on the head with a heavy walking cane
Who: A middle-aged dentist in heavy debt
Detail: Someone had videotaped the murder

Murder Scene #411

Where: The victim was found in a pond
How: Stabbed in the stomach with a dagger
Who: A fire investigator working on a case
Detail: Something is missing from the victim's wallet

Murder Scene #412

Where: The body was found in a hotel resort
How: Beheaded with a hatchet
Who: A hotel manager who lied to his employer
Detail: The victim has a red line on his stomach

Murder Scene #413

Where: The deceased was found inside a zoo cage
How: Bitten to death by a tiger
Who: A socialite who lost all her money
Detail: A witness is lying

Murder Scene #414

Where: The victim was found on a cruise ship
How: Clobbered to death with a heavy ash tray
Who: A short-tempered physics professor
Detail: The victm's wet footprints stopped twenty feet away from the body

Murder Scene #415

Where: The victim was found in a car
How: Stabbed in the eye with a butter knife
Who: A young motel desk clerk
Detail: A missing room key is involved

Murder Scene #416

Where: The victim was found in a movie theatre
How: Strangled by a wire
Who: A fire inspector who was acquitted of a criminal case some years ago
Detail: There was something suspicious about the popcorn

Murder Scene #417

Where: The deceased was found in the lift shaft
How: Hung to death from an electrical cable
Who: An air stewardess who suspected her boyfriend of cheating on her
Detail: Someone saw the victim dashing out of her home

Murder Scene #418

Where: The deceased was found in a locked car
How: Death from heatstroke
Who: A TV talk show host facing a lawsuit
Detail: The victim was tied and gagged

Murder Scene #419

Where: The deceased was found in the backseat of a luxury car
How: Mercury poisoning
Who: An opera singer transporting something illegal
Detail: A family member noticed the victim in distress the day before

Murder Scene #420

Where: The body was found in his study room
How: Stabbed in the eye with a steak knife
Who: A software engineer with a gambling problem
Detail: A witness overheard the victim having an angry phone conversation with someone

Murder Scene #421

Where: The deceased was found in the shower
How: Massive blood loss caused by slitting of wrist
Who: A truck driver who recently came into an inheritance
Detail: The scene of the crime was unusually hot

Murder Scene #422

Where: The body was found on a hotel bed
How: Throat cut by broken shards from a glass
Who: A preschool teacher in deep depression
Detail: There is a rip in the victim's shirt

Murder Scene #423

Where: The deceased was found in a ballroom
How: Stabbed in the head with a sharp stiletto shoe
Who: A celebrity with a fetish
Detail: The victim's water was drugged

Murder Scene #424

Where: The victim was found in a church
How: Bludgeoned to death with a candlestick
Who: A well-respected marine engineer
Detail: The blood splatters on the walls do not match up

Murder Scene #425

Where: The deceased was found in a library
How: Killed by a falling bookshelf
Who: A library consultant with family trouble
Detail: The victim's hand is frozen in an odd gesture

Murder Scene #426

Where: The body was found in a hospital
How: Cocaine intoxication
Who: A well-known pediatric dentist
Detail: The victim had left behind a note

Murder Scene #427

Where: The victim was found in a hotel kitchen
How: Clobbered to death with a wok
Who: A homeless man with family trouble
Detail: The murder took place after closing hours

Murder Scene #428

Where: The victim was found in a flour mill
How: Broken neck from a falling sack of flour
Who: A customs inspector who took bribes
Detail: A burnt locket was found at the crime scene

Murder Scene #429

Where: The victim was found in an ancient tomb
How: Head struck by a heavy object
Who: An archaeologist about to reveal an important find to the press
Detail: The victim died pointing to something on the wall

Murder Scene #430

Where: The body was found in a cruise ship
How: Strangled with a whip
Who: A historical archivist who was being threatened
Detail: A lipstick mark was found on the victim's shirt

Murder Scene #431

Where: The body was found in a private boys' school
How: Signs of being buried alive in concrete
Who: A promising professor
Detail: The victim's tie is tied the wrong way

Murder Scene #432

Where: The deceased was found in a crate in the woods
How: Bitten to death by a ferocious animal
Who: A gifted artist with a secret
Detail: There is something odd about the bite marks

Murder Scene #433

Where: The victim was found at home
How: Struck on the head with a cast iron pan
Who: A casino employee who was engaged in corporate espionage
Detail: The victim's shirt is tucked the wrong way

Murder Scene #434

Where: The victim was found in a top secret laboratory
How: Arsenic poisoning
Who: A medical lab director who likes to drink heavily
Detail: A witness overheard the victim having an angry phone conversation with someone

Murder Scene #435

Where: The body was found in the forest
How: Strangled with underwear
Who: A rental clerk who lied to his bosses
Detail: There are red scars on the victim's neck

Murder Scene #436

Where: The deceased was found in an abandoned car at the harbour
How: Carbon monoxide poisoning
Who: A used car dealer
Detail: The victim's feet were tied together

Murder Scene #437

Where: The victim was found in a petrol station washroom
How: Choked to death on toilet soap
Who: A politician with a penchant for fast cars
Detail: A witness saw the murderer's back view

Murder Scene #438

Where: The victim was found in a bathroom
How: Suffocated with a large sausage forced down the throat
Who: A university professor with a fetish
Detail: Something is abnormal about the victim's fingers

Murder Scene #439

Where: The victim was found at a gravestone in the cemetery
How: Poison on gravestone
Who: A tenor who likes to keep to himself
Detail: There was a strong smell of perfume at the crime scene

Murder Scene #440

Where: The victim was found in the deep woods
How: Bitten by a black mamba
Who: A baker who was involved in a robbery heist a decade ago
Detail: The victim was wearing thick clothing in the hot weather

Murder Scene #441

Where: The deceased was found in the boot of a car
How: Starvation
Who: An unpopular teacher
Detail: The soles of the victim's shoes are muddy

Murder Scene #442

Where: The body was found in a carpentry workshop
How: Smothered to death in sawdust
Who: A worker who lost all his money
Detail: There was no sign of a struggle

Murder Scene #443

Where: The body was found in a corporate boardroom
How: Drug overdose
Who: A teenage pop singer who discovered a secret
Detail: The victim scrawled a message before he died

Murder Scene #444

Where: The victim was found in the backseat of a cab
How: Stabbed in the neck with a nail
Who: A mild criminal investigator who does something peculiar every afternoon
Detail: There is a black stain on the victim's fingernail

Murder Scene #445

Where: The victim was found in a plane hangar
How: Head bashed in with a spanner
Who: A technician who was harbouring a criminal
Detail: The door of the crime scene was locked from the inside

Murder Scene #446

Where: The body was found inside an office cubicle
How: Poison on a drinking straw
Who: A resentful psychiatrist who was going to resign from his job
Detail: The victim tore something up before he died

Murder Scene #447

Where: The deceased was found inside a sauna
How: Steamed to death
Who: A domineering soccer star
Detail: The victim's towel has a faint stain on it

Murder Scene #448

Where: The body was found in a plane washroom
How: Suffocated to death
Who: A prominent tycoon in the middle of a sex scandal
Detail: There was a strong smell of alcohol on the victim's body

Murder Scene #449

Where: The deceased was found in an attic
How: Struck on the head by a golf club
Who: An exhibit artist with a dark family past
Detail: A witness overheard the victim having an angry phone conversation with someone

Murder Scene #450

Where: The deceased was found hidden inside a bale of straw
How: Trampled to death by a horse
Who: An evangelist whose entire life was a lie
Detail: There is a odd smudge at the victim's neck

Murder Scene #451

Where: The body was found under the bed
How: Toxic nail polish
Who: A charismatic news anchor who was involved in a scandal with a politician
Detail: A witness heard the victim complaining about something

Murder Scene #452

Where: The body was found in a publishing house
How: Poisoned ketchup
Who: An editorial director about to retrench the staff
Detail: A witness saw the victim shouting at someone

Murder Scene #453

Where: The deceased was found in a carpark
How: Struck on the head with an icepick
Who: A girl band pop idol with a rival at work
Detail: The weather proves to be the murderer's downfall

Murder Scene #454

Where: The deceased was found buried in the woods
How: Strangled with a belt
Who: A disgruntled coatroom attendant who had seen something he

shouldn't
Detail: A witness saw the victim speaking secretively to someone

Murder Scene #455

Where: The victim was found in a bank vault
How: Stabbed in the stomach with a knife
Who: A paranoid banker
Detail: The victim's home had been burned to the ground

Murder Scene #456

Where: The deceased was found in the middle of the road
How: Broken neck from falling from a great height
Who: A drug dealer who wanted out
Detail: There is a cut on the victim's neck

Murder Scene #457

Where: The victim was found on the rooftop of a skyscraper
How: Strangled by an electrical cord
Who: A chemistry professor who suspected his wife of cheating on him
Detail: The murder took place in the heat of summer

Murder Scene #458

Where: The deceased was found in a beauty salon
How: Suffocated with a wig stuffed down the throat
Who: A highly esteemed engineering manager with enemies
Detail: The victim's ankles were duct taped together

Murder Scene #459

Where: The victim was found in a crate
How: Signs of being buried alive
Who: A rookie cop who lied about her past
Detail: A witness saw the victim shouting at someone

Murder Scene #460

Where: The deceased was found at home
How: Mauled to death by a large dog
Who: A medical student about to release a research paper

Detail: Someone witnessed the victim destroying some papers

Murder Scene #461

Where: The body was found in a van
How: Suffocated to death with nose and mouth sealed by industrial strength glue
Who: A mining engineer who lied about his past
Detail: The victim has been dead for over a year

Murder Scene #462

Where: The body was found in a tar pit
How: Electrocuted
Who: A TV personality who had undergone plastic surgery
Detail: There was a map in the victim's pocket

Murder Scene #463

Where: The body was found in an underground bunker
How: Fatal allergic reaction to fumes
Who: Daughter of a steel magnate
Detail: The victim had unexplainable bruises on her forearm

Murder Scene #464

Where: The body was found on a busy street
How: Crushed to death by a toppling vending machine
Who: An occupational therapist in a dispute with a client
Detail: A broken watch was found at the crime scene

Murder Scene #465

Where: The body was found in a river bed
How: Poisoned sandwich
Who: A middle-aged history professor
Detail: The victim's clothes are missing

Murder Scene #466

Where: The body was found in the boot of a car
How: Strangled by rope
Who: An automotive engineer facing a lawsuit

Detail: The victim's shoelace is missing

Murder Scene #467

Where: The deceased was found outside a restaurant
How: Throat torn out by what seems to a large animal bite
Who: A well regarded restaurant cook
Detail: A broken shoe was found near the crime scene

Murder Scene #468

Where: The deceased was found inside an abandoned house
How: Struck in the stomach with an axe
Who: A perfectionist history professor who is an alcoholic
Detail: The victim's clothes are wet

Murder Scene #469

Where: The victim was found in an alleyway
How: Burnt to death with kerosene
Who: A college professor who betrayed his wife
Detail: There is a yellow powder-like substance around the body

Murder Scene #470

Where: The deceased was found in a lagoon
How: Bitten by a sea snake
Who: A songwriter in the middle of a sex scandal
Detail: A witness has tampered with the evidence

Murder Scene #471

Where: The body was found at a construction site
How: Stabbed with a knife
Who: An elderly camp director who had gone missing a week ago
Detail: There was a video recording of the murder

Murder Scene #472

Where: The body was found in the lobby of an apartment building
How: Beaten to death with a heavy lamp
Who: A survey researcher who lied to his bosses
Detail: A stash of secret photos was found in the victim's home

Murder Scene #473

Where: The body was found on the rooftop of a hospital
How: Strangled to death with dental floss
Who: A child support investigator with a mysterious past
Detail: There was a ransom note stuffed in the victim's pocket

Murder Scene #474

Where: The body was found inside an antique cabinet
How: Struck in the stomach with a crossbow arrow
Who: A politician with marriage problems
Detail: Something is abnormal about the victim's mouth

Murder Scene #475

Where: The body was found on a golf course
How: Poisoned glove
Who: A corrupt goverment official
Detail: Someone received a call from the murderer after the victim was killed

Murder Scene #476

Where: The body was found in a lift
How: Gunshot wound to the head
Who: A smooth-talking paparazzi
Detail: Some photos are missing from the victim's briefcase

Murder Scene #477

Where: The victim was found in a fish farm
How: Decapitated by a wire
Who: A fish farmer who was hiding something that happened two decades ago
Detail: The victim received an odd message on his mobile phone before he died

Murder Scene #478

Where: The body was found in a radio station
How: Cyanide poisoning

Who: A well-known radio producer
Detail: There is a strong smell at the crime scene

Murder Scene #479

Where: The deceased was found in a pub
How: Throat slit by broken glass
Who: A well-liked waitress with a distinctive tattoo on her body
Detail: The victim has a burn mark on her shoulder

Murder Scene #480

Where: The victim was found in the washroom of a pub
How: A gunshot wound in the head
Who: A corporate CEO about to sign a large contract
Detail: The murderer had an accomplice

Murder Scene #481

Where: The body was found in an opera box
How: Struck on the head by a heavy flower piece
Who: A theatre critic with a reputation for womanizing
Detail: The victim has a bruise on his forearm

Murder Scene #482

Where: The victim was found in an abandoned boat by the river
How: Bludgeoned to death with a crowbar
Who: A childcare worker facing a lawsuit
Detail: Something is missing from the victim's belongings

Murder Scene #483

Where: The body was found in a private girls' school
How: Poisoned cake
Who: A domineering valedictorian with a secret
Detail: The victim has a red line on her forehead

Murder Scene #484

Where: The body was found inside a workshop
How: Broken neck from a heavy falling object
Who: A highly respected toy model maker

Detail: The victim's shirt has a faint stain on it

Murder Scene #485

Where: The deceased was found in his bedroom
How: Throat cut by a broken mirror piece
Who: A Oscar winning actor facing a divorce
Detail: There were drops of liquor around the body

Murder Scene #486

Where: The body was found in the middle of the road
How: Pushed into the path of an incoming car
Who: An outspoken police officer who was planning to resign
Detail: A witness noticed the victim in tears the day before

Murder Scene #487

Where: The deceased was found at his workplace canteen
How: Poisoned mustard
Who: A bus driver who suspected his wife of cheating on him
Detail: A witness heard the victim complaining about something

Murder Scene #488

Where: The body was found in a horse stable
How: Electrocuted to death
Who: A fashion model in a family dispute
Detail: The victim had been dead for over a week

Murder Scene #489

Where: The victim was found on the railway tracks in an underground tunnel
How: Struck on the throat with an axe
Who: A medical technologist embroiled in a corporate scandal
Detail: The weather proves to be the murderer's downfall

Murder Scene #490

Where: The body was found in an airport
How: Strangled to death from bare heads
Who: An automotive engineer with designs on his wife's wealth

Detail: A mark on the victim's neck may provide a clue to the murderer's identity

Murder Scene #491

Where: The body was found in the washroom of a train
How: Knife stab in the stomach
Who: An fraud investigator with a family secret
Detail: There was a map in the victim's pocket

Murder Scene #492

Where: The body was found in a military camp
How: Bludgeoned to death with a crowbar
Who: A ruthless espionage intelligence agent
Detail: The victim had left behind a coded message

Murder Scene #493

Where: The deceased was found in a radio station
How: Bitten by a six-eyed sand spider
Who: A professional boxer about to reveal something to the press
Detail: Someone witnessed the victim berating someone furiously

Murder Scene #494

Where: The deceased was found under a bridge
How: Beheaded
Who: A pessimistic jewel thief who had seen something he shouldn't
Detail: The murder took place in the heat of summer

Murder Scene #495

Where: The victim was found in a concrete mixer
How: Struck on the head by a rifle
Who: A famed sociology professor who held the key to a secret
Detail: The victim was grabbing at something before he died

Murder Scene #496

Where: The body was found in a dance studio
How: Struck on the head with an icepick
Who: A cocky dance teacher with a rival at work

Detail: The victim's hands were tied behind his back

Murder Scene #497

Where: The victim was found in an all-boys boarding school
How: Poisoned toothpaste
Who: A star student who was rumoured to be of royal lineage
Detail: The victim was wearing only one contact lens

Murder Scene #498

Where: The body was found in a hotel toilet
How: Hung to death from the window
Who: A freight agent who was two-timing her boyfriend
Detail: There is a deep cut on the victim's thigh

Murder Scene #499

Where: The victim was found in a car crash
How: Died of massive blood loss
Who: A combat engineer with a rival at work
Detail: The victim's hands were tied to the steering wheel

Murder Scene #500

Where: The body was found in his apartment
How: Suffocation to death from dry ice smoke
Who: A finance controller with jealous rivals
Detail: A witness saw the victim exchanging suitcases with someone on the street

HOW TO USE THE AMAZING MURDER SCENE GENERATOR

The Amazing Murder Scene Generator is divided into five sections, A to E. Each section contains a list of possible settings, characters and circumstances.

You need to pick one random number for each of the sections:

A. Where was the victim found?
Pick a number between 1 - 360.

B. How did the victim die?
Pick a number between 1 - 350.

C. Who was the victim?
Pick a number between 1 - 660.

D. What circumstances was the victim in?
Pick a number between 1 - 210.

E. Wild card detail.
Pick a number between 1 - 300.

The murder scene write-up structure is as follows:

Where: The body was found **A**
How: **B**
Who: **C** and **D**
Detail: **E**

For example, if you had picked the following numbers for each of the sections:

Where: The body was found **A122**
How: **B45**
Who: **C472** and **D10**
Detail: **E34**

You would have the the following murder scene scenario:

Where: The body was found **at the bottom of a well**
How: **Stabbed in the eye with a knitting needle**
Who: **A music teacher with family trouble**
Detail: **The victim's ankles were duct taped together**

If you are reading this on a Kindle, you can search for the number directly (e.g. "A122") with the Kindle search document function, instead of scrolling through the lists. You can generate murder scenes much faster this way. I hope you enjoy using the Amazing Murder Scene Generator for your stories!

THE AMAZING MURDER SCENE GENERATOR

A. WHERE WAS THE VICTIM FOUND?

A1. In the living room
A2. In the bedroom
A3. In the drawing room
A4. In the lobby
A5. In a corridor
A6. In the toilet
A7. In a hotel toilet
A8. In a lift lobby
A9. In the bathtub
A10. On a hotel roof
A11. In a stairwell
A12. In a car
A13. By the roadside
A14. In the forest
A15. In a chimney
A16. Under the bed
A17. In a closet
A18. In a fridge
A19. In a crate
A20. In a boat
A21. In a yacht
A22. In a chest
A23. In the sea
A24. In a classroom
A25. On stage
A26. In a ballroom
A27. In a pond
A28. In a swimming pool
A29. In the boot of a car
A30. In the carpark
A31. In a military bunker
A32. In a swamp
A33. In an ice box
A34. In a plane
A35. On a balcony
A36. In the kitchen
A37. In a wall
A38. In an opera box

A39. In a movie theatre
A40. In a sports stadium
A41. In a theatre dressing room
A42. In a greenhouse
A43. In a photography studio
A44. In a river
A45. In a stream
A46. Under a bridge
A47. In the basement of a house
A48. In a shop basement
A49. In a shopping mall
A50. Inside an ice block
A51. In a walk-in freezer
A52. On a lamp post
A53. In a helicopter
A54. In a cruise ship
A55. On a tree
A56. On a train
A57. In an underground tunnel
A58. In the sewer
A59. In a septic tank
A60. In a lake
A61. On a railway
A62. On the roof top of a train
A63. In the washroom of a train
A64. In the washroom of a plane
A65. Inside an office cubicle
A66. Inside a cargo crate on a plane
A67. On the railway tracks in an underground tunnel
A68. Propped against the door
A69. Inside an abandoned house
A70. In a graveyard
A71. On the cemetery gates
A72. In a drain
A73. Over a fence
A74. In a schoolyard
A75. In a backyard
A76. Hanging in a waterfall
A77. Hanging from a cliff
A78. On a cliff
A79. At the bottom of a cliff
A80. Hanging from a window
A81. Hanging from a bridge

A82. On the bonnet of a car
A83. Under a car
A84. In a rescue float in the sea
A85. Inside a zoo cage
A86. Inside a musuem
A87. In a fun ride in the amusement park
A88. In a playground
A89. Inside a dumpster
A90. On a soccer pitch
A91. Inside a tour agency office
A92. Buried in quicksand
A93. In a hospital bed
A94. In a hospital operating theater
A95. In a hospital ultrasound room
A96. In a dental clinic
A97. In a restaurant kitchen
A98. In a hotel restaurant kitchen
A99. In a toy shop
A100. In a clothing shop
A101. In a chocolate shop
A102. In a shoe shop
A103. In a wax musuem
A104. In a bakery
A105. In an eatery
A106. In a government office
A107. On a factory floor
A108. In a fire station
A109. In a fire engine
A110. In a warehouse
A111. Inside the wheel well of a plane
A112. In a film studio
A113. On a film set
A114. In a stock exchange
A115. In a printing house
A116. In a petrol station
A117. In a coffee shop
A118. In a gentleman's club
A119. On a golf course
A120. In a carpentry workshop
A121. On a ship mast
A122. At the bottom of a well
A123. Inside a community centre
A124. In a university lecture hall

A125. In a public restroom
A126. In a recording studio
A127. In a military camp
A128. In a press room
A129. In a church
A130. In a factory vat
A131. In a school principal's office
A132. In a student dormitory
A133. In a male student dormitory
A134. In a female student dormitory
A135. In a professor's office
A136. Underwater in a tourist attraction
A137. In a dye vat
A138. Inside a tour bus
A139. Inside a hotel room
A140. In a corporate boardroom
A141. Inside a vending machine
A142. Inside a vet clinic
A143. In a brothel
A144. In a top secret laboratory
A145. In the engine room of a submarine
A146. In the engine room of a ship
A147. Inside a nuclear reactor
A148. In a farm
A149. In a barn
A150. In a pasture
A151. On a cycling path
A152. In a field of wheat
A153. In the cockpit of an air plane
A154. In a drug shelter
A155. In an ambulance
A156. In an animal shelter
A157. In a kennel
A158. In a cave
A159. In an alleyway
A160. In a call center
A161. In an archeology site
A162. In a tomb
A163. In a badminton court
A164. In a fish farm
A165. In an aquarium
A166. Inside a fish tank
A167. In an armored tank

A168. In an art musuem
A169. On an art exhibit
A170. Inside a gym
A171. Inside a school science lab
A172. Inside a luggage bag
A173. Inside a suitcase
A174. Inside an oven
A175. In a bank
A176. In a bicycle repair workshop
A177. In a gun firing range
A178. In a publishing house
A179. In a television studio
A180. In an abandoned building
A181. In an abandoned mansion
A182. In a dry swimming pool
A183. Under a bulldozer
A184. In a bulldozer
A185. Under a bus
A186. Inside an antique cabinet
A187. In a camping site
A188. In a casino
A189. Under the floorboards
A190. In a cloakroom
A191. In a doctor's waiting room
A192. In a dentist's waiting room
A193. In a locker room
A194. In a changing room
A195. In a dressing room
A196. In a construction site
A197. In a fast food outlet
A198. In the kitchen of a fast food outlet
A199. In a lawyer's office
A200. In a hair salon
A201. In a beauty salon
A202. In a video rental shop
A203. On a motorbike
A204. Hanging from a crane
A205. In a guard house
A206. In a tailor shop
A207. In a van
A208. In a caravan van
A209. In a radio station
A210. On a horse

A211. On a horse racing track
A212. On a car racing track
A213. In the lift shaft
A214. At the bottom of an elevator shaft
A215. In a public library
A216. In a nature reserve
A217. In a resort
A218. In a private boys' school
A219. In a private girls' school
A220. In a forensic science lab
A221. In a mortuary
A222. On a forklift
A223. In a funeral parlor
A224. In an open coffin
A225. Hidden inside a couch
A226. Hidden inside a statue
A227. Hidden inside a bale of straw
A228. In a slaughter house
A229. In a dairy farm
A230. In a cornfield
A231. In a high school
A232. In a motel
A233. In a landfill
A234. In a refuse dump
A235. Inside a mailroom
A236. In a meat packing factory
A237. In a medical school
A238. In a flour mill
A239. Inside a mine
A240. In a music room
A241. Inside a fountain
A242. In a garden nursery
A243. In a parking lot
A244. On a tennis court
A245. On a basketball court
A246. In an indoor swimming pool
A247. In a student hostel
A248. In a retail store
A249. At a pier
A250. In a canal
A251. Inside a grandfather clock
A252. Under a tree
A253. On a public statue

A254. In an underground bunker
A255. In a lake
A256. By a lake
A257. By a lamp post
A258. On a bridge
A259. By a garden path
A260. In a temple
A261. In an airport
A262. In an airfield
A263. In a police station
A264. In a bank vault
A265. In a park
A266. In a shed
A267. In a garden shed
A268. In a shack
A269. Inside a tent
A270. On a Ferris wheel
A271. In an observatory science centre
A272. On a hillside
A273. In a lighthouse
A274. At the seashore
A275. At the bottom of a mountain
A276. On a hiking trail
A277. In a mountain valley
A278. In a washroom
A279. In a bell tower
A280. In a subway
A281. In a hostel washroom
A282. In a hostel lounge
A283. In a storeroom
A284. In an office pantry
A285. In a dance studio
A286. In a dance hall
A287. In a bar
A288. In a pub
A289. In the washroom of a pub
A290. In the washroom of a bar
A291. In an abandoned boat by the river
A292. In the reeds by the river
A293. In the centre of the city square
A294. At the bottom of a lake
A295. At the bottom of a river
A296. In a wine cellar

A297. In an attic
A298. On the rooftop of a skyscraper
A299. On the rooftop of a hospital
A300. In an abandoned car on a dirt road
A301. By a dirt road
A302. On a swing
A303. In a cab
A304. Inside a block of ice
A305. Inside a block of cement
A306. At the harbour
A307. In a tar pit
A308. Off a desolated road
A309. In a private boarding school
A310. In an all-boys boarding school
A311. In an all-girls boarding school
A312. In a garbage bin
A313. In a river bed
A314. In a church pew
A315. In a plane hangar
A316. In a horse stable
A317. In a gas station shop
A318. In a train station terminal
A319. In a concert venue
A320. In an evacuation centre
A321. In a boiler
A322. In a candy shop
A323. In a timber mill
A324. In the deep woods
A325. In a concrete mixer
A326. In the backseat of a luxury car
A327. On the bonnet of a car
A328. In an airplane
A329. In a dentist's chair
A330. In a monastery
A331. In a luxury home
A332. In a hotel lounge
A333. On his/her bed
A334. In his/her office
A335. On a hotel bed
A336. In a television studio
A337. In a golf course
A338. In a crate in the woods
A339. In his/her study room

A340. At the foot of an apartment building
A341. On a soccer pitch
A342. In a retail store after closing hours
A343. In the driver's seat of a car
A344. In a motorbike crash
A345. In a car crash
A346. In the shower
A347. Buried in the woods
A348. In the lobby of an apartment building
A349. In a cable car
A350. In an abandoned factory
A351. In an art studio
A352. At his/her office desk
A353. In a field of corn
A354. In the boot of an abandoned car
A355. In a casino
A356. In a hotel kitchen
A357. In an ancient tomb
A358. Inside a sauna
A359. In his/her apartment
A360. At his/her workplace canteen

B. HOW DID THE VICTIM DIE?

B1. Boiled to death
B2. Skinned alive
B3. Strangled by rope
B4. Eaten by an animal
B5. Struck on the head with a heavy walking cane
B6. Multiple gunshot wounds
B7. Multiple slash wounds
B8. Snake bite
B9. Poison
B10. Stabbed in the eye with a pen
B11. Strangled by a dog leash
B12. Drowning
B13. Stabbed in the eye with an icepick
B14. Strangled by bare hands
B15. Dismembered alive by saw
B16. Bitten by a sea snake
B17. Dismembered alive by hatchet
B18. Stabbed in the chest with a pitchfork
B19. Dismembered alive by machete
B20. Throat torn out by what seems to a large animal bite
B21. Stabbed in the eye with a sharpened toothbrush
B22. Struck in the stomach with a crossbow arrow
B23. Stabbed in the chest with a knife
B24. Dismembered alive by chainsaw
B25. Strangled by hair
B26. Bludgeoned to death with a baseball bat
B27. Broken neck by falling luggage
B28. Fatal allergic reaction to mold
B29. Strangled by bedsheets
B30. Stabbed in the back with a dagger
B31. Strangled by a computer mouse cord
B32. Multiple stab wounds
B33. Stabbed in the eye with a dagger
B34. Strangled by pantyhose
B35. Battered to death with a golf club
B36. Cocaine intoxication
B37. Decapitated by a wire
B38. Stomped to death
B39. Strangled by wire
B40. Stabbed in the eye with a corkscrew
B41. Starvation

B42. Bomb explosion
B43. Stabbed in the eye with a BBQ skewer
B44. Strangled by a shoelace
B45. Stabbed in the eye with a knitting needle
B46. Fatal allergic reaction to seafood
B47. Attacked by wolves
B48. Struck on the head with a hammer
B49. Stabbed in the back with an icepick
B50. Struck on the head by a manual typewriter
B51. Crushed by a falling sandbag
B52. Gored by a cow
B53. Struck on the head by a toilet tank lid
B54. Toxic clothing
B55. Stabbed in the throat with a fire poker
B56. Throat slit by a blade
B57. Struck on the head by a boomerang
B58. Lead poisoning
B59. Dismembered alive by axe
B60. Hung to death from a noose
B61. Struck on the head with a cast iron pan
B62. Struck in the stomach with an axe
B63. Stabbed in the eye with a syringe
B64. A gunshot wound in the chest
B65. Stabbed in the eye with a long hairpin
B66. Stabbed in the stomach with a knife
B67. Dehydration
B68. Throat slit by broken glass
B69. Stabbed in the eye with a knife
B70. Strangled by an electrical cord
B71. Trampled by a horse
B72. Gored by hogs
B73. Attacked by a tiger shark
B74. Bludgeoned to death with a hammer
B75. Stabbed in the chest with a fire poker
B76. Struck in the stomach with a crossbow arrow
B77. Stabbed in the throat with a samurai sword
B78. Beaten to death
B79. Steamed to death
B80. Bludgeoned to death with a candlestick
B81. Strangled by curtains
B82. Struck on the back with an axe
B83. Stabbed in the stomach with a dagger
B84. A gunshot wound in the head

B85. Stabbed in the stomach with a samurai sword
B86. Struck on the head by a falling slab of concrete
B87. Stabbed in the back with a fire poker
B88. Brain swelling caused by massive consumption of water
B89. Crushed by a falling statue
B90. Lethal injection of poison
B91. Toxic hair dye
B92. Stabbed in the stomach with a fire poker
B93. Toxic makeup
B94. Burnt alive
B95. Methanol poisoning
B96. Attacked by an anaconda
B97. Stabbed in the stomach with a kitchen knife
B98. Struck on the head with an icepick
B99. Crushed by falling rubble
B100. Stabbed in the throat with an icepick
B101. Struck on the head by a brick
B102. Struck on the head with a frozen leg of ham
B103. Fatal injuries consistent from having fallen from a great height
B104. Carbon monoxide poisoning
B105. Stabbed in the stomach with an icepick
B106. Arsenic poisoning
B107. Crushed by a falling monument
B108. Hypothermia
B109. Struck on the head by a falling flowerpot
B110. Struck on the head with an axe
B111. Anthrax poisoning
B112. Fatal allergic reaction to shellfish
B113. Suffocation to death with plaster around the head
B114. Struck on the head with an ice block
B115. Fatal allergic reaction to perfume
B116. Struck on the head by falling luggage
B117. Broken neck by a falling ice block
B118. Struck on the head with a fire poker
B119. Crushed by a falling tree
B120. Struck on the throat with an axe
B121. Stung to death by fire ants
B122. Stabbed in the head with a sharp stiletto shoe
B123. Suffocation to death with a pillow
B124. Throat slit by a wire
B125. Stabbed in the eye with a razor blade
B126. Attacked by a pet ape
B127. Broken neck by a falling sandbag

B128. Struck on the head with a cleaver
B129. Throat slit by a razor blade
B130. Struck on the head by a heavy ashtray
B131. Shot in the head by a nailgun
B132. Multiple injuries in head from a drill
B133. Fatal allergic reaction to a bee sting
B134. Bitten to death by army ants
B135. Struck in the stomach with a crossbow arrow
B136. Stabbed in the head with a corkscrew
B137. Warfarin poisoning
B138. Throat slit by a dagger
B139. Signs of being buried alive
B140. Crushed by a falling chandelier
B141. Struck on the throat with a cleaver
B142. Bludgeoned to death with a crowbar
B143. Fatal allergic reaction to a hornet sting
B144. Strangled by ribbons
B145. Oleander poisoning
B146. Stabbed in the chest with an icepick
B147. Bitten by a black mamba
B148. Stabbed in the eye with a scalpel
B149. Massive blood loss caused by slitting of wrist
B150. Stabbed in the back with a knife
B151. A gunshot wound in the eye
B152. Struck on the head by falling rubble
B153. Throat slit by a samurai sword
B154. Yew poisoning
B155. Gored by wild boars
B156. Poisoned pasta
B157. Bitten by a yellow sac spider
B158. Poisoned toothbrush
B159. Suffocated to death by a python
B160. Bitten to death by wild dogs
B161. Eaten alive by rats
B162. Strychnine poisoning
B163. Attacked by piranhas
B164. Fatal allergic reaction to a wasp sting
B165. Nicotine poisoning
B166. Stung to death by hornets
B167. Drug overdose
B168. Fatal allergic reaction to antibiotics
B169. Stung to death by wasps
B170. Beheaded with an axe

B171. Toxic gloves
B172. Lye poisoning
B173. Trampled by an elephant
B174. Beheaded with a wire
B175. Mercury poisoning
B176. Toxic socks
B177. Bitten by a six-eyed sand spider
B178. Knife stab in the stomach
B179. Air bubble in the artery
B180. Beheaded
B181. Poison on dollar notes
B182. Bitten by a puff adder
B183. Electrocution
B184. Cyanide poisoning
B185. Crushed in a waste compactor
B186. Blowfish poisoning
B187. Bitten by a king cobra
B188. Beheaded with a hatchet
B189. Poisoned bandaid
B190. Stabbed in the eye with a steak knife
B191. Bitten by a tarantula spider
B192. Poison on the screen of a mobile phone
B193. Fatal allergic reaction to peanuts
B194. Poison on a drinking straw
B195. Stung to death by bees
B196. Beheaded with a cleaver
B197. Bitten by a great white shark
B198. Poisoned wine glass
B199. Bitten by a redback spider
B200. Poison on the pages of a book
B201. Strangled by a jump rope
B202. Knife stab in the eye
B203. Attacked by a crocodile
B204. Toxic underwear
B205. Run over by a car
B206. Died from injuries consistent with a car crash
B207. Poisoned water
B208. Drowned in a toilet bowl
B209. Throat cut by a broken DVD
B210. Poisoned coffee
B211. Poisoned tea
B212. Fatal allergic reaction to sunlight
B213. Poisoned nail polish

B214. Stabbed in the eye with a chopstick
B215. Fatal allergic reaction to wheat
B216. Poisoned beer
B217. Stabbed in the eye with a fork
B218. Struck on the head by a heavy vase
B219. Toxic wallpaper
B220. Bitten by a rattlesnake
B221. Beheaded with a samurai sword
B222. Poisoned wine
B223. Head struck by a bathroom scale
B224. Poisoned toothpaste
B225. Crushed in a car crusher
B226. Poisoned mug
B227. Fatal allergic reaction to latex
B228. Polonium poisoning
B229. Killed by a falling bookshelf
B230. Drowned in a sink
B231. Scalded to death in a hot shower
B232. Suffocated to death with nose and mouth sealed by industrial strength glue
B233. Poisoned mustard
B234. Choked to death on ball bearings
B235. Suffocated to death by a vacuum cleaner in the mouth
B236. Throat cut by a broken mirror piece
B237. Crushed by a microwave
B238. Injection with poison from an umbrella
B239. Fatal sting from scorpion
B240. Smothered to death with a mop
B241. Injection with poison from a pen
B242. Clobbered to death with a rolling pin
B243. Bitten by a green mamba
B244. Strangled to death with the electrical cable of a toaster
B245. Fatal allergic reaction to oatmeal
B246. Poisoned hair spray
B247. Crushed by falling money
B248. Stabbed in the neck several times with a pen
B249. Poisoned BBQ skewers
B250. Smothered to death with an oven mitt
B251. Throttled to death with a bath towel
B252. Poisoned smoke
B253. Smothered to death with a cushion
B254. Thallium sulfate poisoning
B255. Clobbered to death with a toaster

B256. Throat cut by shattered glass from a shower door
B257. Poisoned cake
B258. Crushed to death by a toppling refrigerator
B259. Beaten to death with a broom
B260. Whipped to death with an electrical cable
B261. Poisoned hair comb
B262. Crushed to death by an avalanche of trash
B263. Head struck by a TV set
B264. Ricin poisoning
B265. Clobbered to death with a bathroom scale
B266. Beaten to death with a heavy lamp
B267. Head struck by a heavy lamp
B268. Poisoned cigarette
B269. Fatal allergic reaction to eggs
B270. Bitten by a black widow spider
B271. Stabbed in the eye with a butter knife
B272. Poisoned ketchup
B273. Suffocated with bread stuffed down the throat
B274. Fatal allergic reaction to pollen
B275. Struck on the head with a heavy wooden cutting board
B276. Poisoned by antifreeze
B277. Forced ingestion of windshield washer fluid
B278. Death from inhalation of deadly chloramine gas
B279. Head bashed in with a guitar
B280. Crushed to death by an electronic gate
B281. Fell from a highway
B282. Crushed to death by a toppling vending machine
B283. Burnt to death with a blow torch
B284. Suffocated by kitty litter
B285. Poisoned candy wrapper
B286. Burnt alive with kerosene
B287. Stabbed in the eye with scissors
B288. Fell from an overhead bridge to the road
B289. Poisoned fingernail
B290. Strangled by a belt
B291. Pushed from a moving car
B292. Poisoned bookmark
B293. Toxic makeup containing arsenic
B294. Kicked to death by zebras
B295. Suffocated with dough stuffed down the throat
B296. Crushed to death by falling meat carcasses
B297. Struck on the head by a falling brick
B298. Strangled by a braid of hair

B299. Fatal allergic reaction to fumes
B300. Dragged to death on the rails behind a moving train
B301. Signs of being buried alive in concrete
B302. Poisoned dental instrument
B303. Stabbed in the throat with a pocket knife
B304. Fatally injured with a stage prop weapon that turned out to be real
B305. Drowned to death in a barrel
B306. Poisoned cocktail
B307. Suffocated to death from low oxygen levels
B308. Poisoned chocolate
B309. Spontaneous combustion
B310. Camera flash triggered gunshot
B311. Death from inhalation of a deadly gas
B312. Poisoned flower pollen
B313. Choked to death on soap
B314. Stabbed through the eye with a bicycle spoke
B315. Poisoned kiss
B316. Pushed into the path of an incoming train
B317. Poisoned mayonnaise
B318. Pushed into the path of an incoming car
B319. Poisoned cutlery
B320. Strangled with underwear
B321. Killed by a soccer ball
B322. Bitten by a ferocious animal
B323. Strangled by a ribbon
B324. Throttled to death by a gym machine
B325. Kicked to death by a horse
B326. Struck on the head by a paperweight
B327. Poisoned oatmeal
B328. Suffocated with a large fish forced down the throat
B329. Strangled by bra strap
B330. Poisoned dart from a blow gun
B331. Beaten to death with a fence plank
B332. Broken neck from a falling sack of concrete
B333. Strangled by a wig
B334. Poisoned toilet paper
B335. Multiple injuries in head from hammered in nails
B336. Poisoned tissue paper
B337. Broken neck from a great fall
B338. Poisoned playing card
B339. Clobbered to death with a tree branch
B340. Crushed by a slab of concrete
B341. Strangled with a whip

B342. Head bashed in with a spanner
B343. Struck on the head by a baseball bat
B344. Smothered to death in sawdust
B345. Strangled to death with dental floss
B346. Suffocation to death from dry ice smoke
B347. Clobbered to death with a wok
B348. Struck on the head by a rifle
B349. Strangled to death from bare heads
B350. Broken neck from a heavy falling object

C. WHO WAS THE VICTIM?

C1. Opera singer
C2. Celebrity
C3. Steel magnate
C4. Drug kingpin
C5. Gangster
C6. Robber
C7. Sailor
C8. Ship captain
C9. Astronaut
C10. Aristocrat
C11. Teenage girl
C12. Teenage boy
C13. Hardened criminal
C14. Drug pusher
C15. Policeman
C16. Cop
C17. Retiree
C18. Restaurant owner
C19. Hotel owner
C20. Socialite
C21. Oscar winning actress
C22. Oscar winning actor
C23. Finance guru
C24. Millionaire
C25. Billionaire
C26. Rock star
C27. Pop idol
C28. Pop singer
C29. Corporate CEO
C30. Professional boxer
C31. Mafia gang leader
C32. Jewel thief
C33. Thief
C34. Used car salesman
C35. Tycoon
C36. Philanthropist
C37. Art collector
C38. Shipping tycoon
C39. Heiress
C40. Heir
C41. Stockbroker

C42. Commodities trader
C43. Senator
C44. Business mogul
C45. Comedian
C46. Catwalk model
C47. Fashion model
C48. Media mogul
C49. Religious leader
C50. Music industry executive
C51. Entrepreneur
C52. Songwriter
C53. TV star
C54. Fashion designer
C55. Investor
C56. TV personality
C57. Radio personality
C58. Record producer
C59. Novelist
C60. Lyricist
C61. Peace activist
C62. Animal rights activist
C63. Human rights activist
C64. Civil rights activist
C65. Government rebel
C66. Terrorist
C67. Refugee
C68. Teenage pop singer
C69. Teenage pop idol
C70. Boy band pop idol
C71. Girl band pop idol
C72. Media personality
C73. Master chef
C74. Late night talk show host
C75. Athlete
C76. Inventor
C77. Theatre actor
C78. Reality television star
C79. Journalist
C80. Combat engineer
C81. Diver
C82. Fire fighter
C83. Special forces officer
C84. Military judge

C85. CID special agent
C86. Military policeman
C87. Dog handler
C88. Animal shelter worker
C89. Drug dealer
C90. Playwright
C91. Evangelist
C92. Prostitute
C93. Professional golfer
C94. Professional gambler
C95. Chemist
C96. Biologist
C97. Academic
C98. Physicist
C99. Government official
C100. Escaped convict
C101. Wanted fugitive
C102. Missionary
C103. Nun
C104. Priest
C105. Women's rights activist
C106. Student
C107. Star student
C108. Prima donna
C109. Cheerleader
C110. Basketball star
C111. Soccer star
C112. Football star
C113. Rugby star
C114. Tennis star
C115. Badminton star
C116. Movie star
C117. Film starlet
C118. Politician
C119. Diplomat
C120. Soprano
C121. Tenor
C122. industrialist
C123. Financer
C124. Superstar
C125. Ballerina
C126. Dancer
C127. Call girl

C128. Businessman
C129. Homeless man
C130. Homeless woman
C131. Runaway bride
C132. Runaway teenager
C133. Widow
C134. Widower
C135. Advertising executive
C136. Housekeeper
C137. Sushi chef
C138. Rookie cop
C139. Hairdresser
C140. Monk
C141. Air pilot
C142. Theatre patroness
C143. Theatre patron
C144. Teaching assistant
C145. Student coordinator
C146. Lighthouse keeper
C147. Archaeologist
C148. Casino employee
C149. Medical lab director
C150. Editorial director
C151. Paparazzi
C152. Seaman
C153. Administrative assistant
C154. Administrative law judge
C155. Adult literacy teacher
C156. Advertising account executive
C157. Aeronautical engineer
C158. Aerospace engineering technician
C159. Farm manager
C160. Air traffic controller
C161. Aircraft cargo handling supervisor
C162. Aircraft examiner
C163. Aircraft mechanic
C164. Airfield operations specialist
C165. Airline flight attendant
C166. Airport administrator
C167. Drug abuse assistance coordinator
C168. Ambulance driver
C169. Amusement park attendant
C170. Anesthesiologist

C171. Animal breeder
C172. Animal control worker
C173. Animal keeper
C174. Animal scientist
C175. Animal trainer
C176. Archeology professor
C177. Anti-terrorism intelligence agent
C178. Soccer referee
C179. Fish farmer
C180. Aquarium curator
C181. Architecture professor
C182. Cultural studies professor
C183. Art director
C184. Art restorer
C185. Art therapist
C186. Music professor
C187. Artists agent
C188. Athletic coach
C189. Athletic director
C190. Athletic trainer
C191. Space scientist
C192. Automobile mechanic
C193. Automotive engineer
C194. Baggage porter
C195. Baker
C196. Ballistics expert
C197. Bank manager
C198. Bank teller
C199. Bicycle mechanic
C200. Biological technician
C201. Biology professor
C202. Biomedical engineer
C203. Boat builder
C204. Book editor
C205. Border patrol agent
C206. Building inspector
C207. Bulldozer operator
C208. Bus mechanic
C209. Truck mechanic
C210. School bus driver
C211. Bus driver
C212. Business professor
C213. Cabinet maker

C214. Camp director
C215. Cardiologist
C216. Career counselor
C217. Freight agent
C218. Cartographer
C219. Cartoonist
C220. Casino cage worker
C221. Casino dealer
C222. Casino manager
C223. Casino pit boss
C224. Casting director
C225. Childcare worker
C226. Prison chaplain
C227. Military chaplain
C228. Hospital chaplain
C229. Chemical engineer
C230. Chemistry professor
C231. Chief financial officer
C232. Child care worker
C233. Child life specialist
C234. Child support investigator
C235. Child support services worker
C236. City planning aide
C237. Civil drafter
C238. Civil engineer
C239. Clergy member
C240. Religious leader
C241. Clinical dietitian
C242. Clinical psychologist
C243. Clinical sociologist
C244. Coatroom attendant
C245. Dressing room attendant
C246. College professor
C247. University professor
C248. Commercial designer
C249. Commercial diver
C250. Commercial fisherman
C251. Community health nurse
C252. Community organization worker
C253. Community welfare worker
C254. Machine tool operator
C255. Computer operator
C256. Computer programmer

C257. Computer science professor
C258. Computer security specialist
C259. Computer software engineer
C260. Computer software technician
C261. Congressional aide
C262. Conservation scientist
C263. Construction driller
C264. Construction labourer
C265. Construction manager
C266. Construction worker
C267. Contract administrator
C268. Contract specialist
C269. Finance controller
C270. Cafeteria cook
C271. Fast food cook
C272. Cook of a private household
C273. Restaurant cook
C274. Short order cook
C275. Copy writer
C276. Corporation lawyer
C277. Correction officer
C278. Correspondence clerk
C279. Hair stylist
C280. Cost accountant
C281. Costume attendant
C282. Counseling psychologist
C283. Rental clerk
C284. City auditor
C285. Courier
C286. Court administrator
C287. Court clerk
C288. Court reporter
C289. Craft artist
C290. Crane operator
C291. Criminal investigator
C292. Detective
C293. Criminal justice professor
C294. Criminal lawyer
C295. Guard
C296. Bespoke tailor
C297. Customs inspector
C298. Database administrator
C299. Deaf students teacher

C300. Delivery driver
C301. Product promoter
C302. Dental office administrator
C303. Dental assistant
C304. Dental hygienist
C305. Dental laboratory technician
C306. Dentist
C307. Dermatologist
C308. Developmental psychologist
C309. Nutritionist
C310. Disabled students teacher
C311. Disk jockey
C312. Dispatcher
C313. Door to door salesman
C314. Economics professor
C315. Editorial writer
C316. Education professor
C317. Educational administrator
C318. Educational psychologist
C319. Educational therapist
C320. Elementary school administrator
C321. Elementary school teacher
C322. Elevator mechanic
C323. Machine assembler
C324. Engineering manager
C325. Engineering professor
C326. Literature professor
C327. Environmental engineer
C328. Executive secretary
C329. Exercise physiologist
C330. Exhibit artist
C331. Exhibit designer
C332. Explosives worker
C333. Factory layout engineer
C334. Family caseworker
C335. Family practitioner
C336. Farm hand
C337. Rancher
C338. Fashion artist
C339. Fashion coordinator
C340. Fashion designer
C341. Fashion model
C342. Fence installer

C343. Field contractor
C344. Field health officer
C345. File clerk
C346. Film editor
C347. Finance manager
C348. Financial aid counselor
C349. Financial analyst
C350. Financial examiner
C351. Financial planner
C352. Fine artist
C353. Fire inspector
C354. Fire investigator
C355. Fishery worker supervisor
C356. Fitness trainer
C357. Flight engineer
C358. Floral designer
C359. Food and drug inspector
C360. Food preparation worker
C361. Food science technicians
C362. Food technologist
C363. Foreign exchange trader
C364. Foreign language interpreter
C365. Foreign language teacher
C366. Foreign language translator
C367. Foreign service officer
C368. Foreign student adviser
C369. Forensic science technician
C370. Forensics psychologist
C371. Forest engineer
C372. Forest fire inspector
C373. Forklift operator
C374. Fraud investigator
C375. Fund raiser
C376. Funeral attendant
C377. Funeral director
C378. Furniture designer
C379. Gas plant operator
C380. Operations manager
C381. General farmworker
C382. Geography professor
C383. Geological data technician
C384. Geological technician
C385. Glass blower

C386. Golf course superintendent
C387. Graduate teaching assistant
C388. Graphic designer
C389. Greenhouse manager
C390. Gynecologist
C391. Harbor master
C392. High school administrator
C393. High school guidance counselor
C394. High school teacher
C395. Highway patrol pilot
C396. Historic site administrator
C397. Historical archivist
C398. History professor
C399. Home economics teacher
C400. Horticulture therapist
C401. Horticulturist
C402. Hospital administrator
C403. Hospital nurse
C404. Hostess
C405. Motel desk clerk
C406. Hotel manager
C407. Hydraulic engineer
C408. Immigration inspector
C409. Industrial designer
C410. Industrial engineer
C411. Infantry officer
C412. Insurance agent
C413. Insurance lawyer
C414. Insurance underwriter
C415. Intelligence specialist
C416. Interior designer
C417. Internal auditor
C418. Interpreter for the hearing impaired
C419. Kindergarten teacher
C420. Land surveyor
C421. Landscape architect
C422. Landscape contractor
C423. Law clerk
C424. Law professor
C425. Legal assistant
C426. Legal secretary
C427. Legislative assistant
C428. Library assistant

C429. Library consultant
C430. Librarian
C431. Loan counselor
C432. Loan interviewer
C433. Loan officer
C434. Locomotive engineer
C435. Mail clerk
C436. Makeup artist
C437. Management consultant
C438. Manicurist
C439. Marine architect
C440. Marine cargo surveyor
C441. Marine drafter
C442. Marine engineer
C443. Marine surveyor
C444. Marketing manager
C445. Marking clerk
C446. Marriage therapist
C447. Massage therapist
C448. Math professor
C449. Meat packer
C450. Mechanical drafter
C451. Mechanical engineer
C452. Public health social worker
C453. Medical illustrator
C454. Medical assistant
C455. Medical secretary
C456. Medical technologist
C457. Mental health counselor
C458. Middle school administrator
C459. Middle school guidance counselor
C460. Middle school teacher
C461. Military analyst
C462. Military officer
C463. Mill worker
C464. Mine inspector
C465. Mining engineer
C466. Missing person investigator
C467. Missionary worker
C468. Model maker
C469. Museum curator
C470. Museum conservator
C471. Music director

C472. Music teacher
C473. Music therapist
C474. Narcotics investigator
C475. Newspaper editor
C476. Magazine writer
C477. Nuclear engineer
C478. Nurse practitioner
C479. Nurse's aide
C480. Nursery worker
C481. Nursing professor
C482. Obstetrician
C483. Occupational physician
C484. Occupational therapist
C485. Occupational therapy assistant
C486. Office clerk
C487. Office supervisor
C488. Operating engineers
C489. Ophthalmologist
C490. Order clerk
C491. Orthodontic assistant
C492. Outdoor education teacher
C493. Parking enforcement officer
C494. Parking lot attendant
C495. Parole officer
C496. Patent agent
C497. Patent lawyer
C498. Pathologist
C499. Payroll clerk
C500. Peace corps worker
C501. Pediatric dentist
C502. Pediatrician
C503. Personnel administrator
C504. Pharmacy aide
C505. Philosophy professor
C506. Physical education instructor
C507. Physical therapist
C508. Physical therapist aide
C509. Physical therapy assistant
C510. Physician's assistant
C511. Physician's office nurse
C512. Physics professor
C513. Commercial airline pilot
C514. Plant breeder

C515. Plastic surgeon
C516. Poet
C517. Police artist
C518. Police officer
C519. Political science professor
C520. Political scientist
C521. Preschool administrator
C522. Preschool teacher
C523. Private investigator
C524. Private nurse
C525. Probation officer
C526. Professional sports scout
C527. Prosthetic technician
C528. Psychiatric aide
C529. Psychiatric technician
C530. Psychiatrist
C531. Psychology professor
C532. Publications editor
C533. Quarry worker
C534. TV announcer
C535. TV news commentator
C536. TV newscaster
C537. TV producer
C538. TV sports announcer
C539. TV talk show host
C540. Radio news commentator
C541. Radio newscaster
C542. Radio producer
C543. Radio sports announcer
C544. Radio talk show host
C545. Rail yard engineer
C546. Railroad conductor
C547. Railroad engineer
C548. Railroad inspector
C549. Real estate appraiser
C550. Real estate assessor
C551. Real estate broker
C552. Real estate lawyer
C553. Recreational therapist
C554. Umpire
C555. Refuse collector
C556. Reservation ticket agent
C557. Residence counselor

C558. Resource teacher
C559. Restaurant manager
C560. Retail salesperson
C561. Retail store manager
C562. Safety inspector
C563. Sales engineer
C564. Sales manager
C565. Sales promoter
C566. Sales representative
C567. School nurse
C568. School psychologist
C569. Screen writer
C570. Script editor
C571. Securities broker
C572. Security guard
C573. Set designer
C574. Set illustrator
C575. Ship carpenter
C576. Ship engineer
C577. Ship master
C578. Ship mate
C579. Ship pilot
C580. Shipping clerk
C581. Community service manager
C582. Social psychologist
C583. Social service volunteer
C584. Social work professor
C585. Social worker
C586. Sociology professor
C587. Soil conservationist
C588. Soil engineer
C589. Soil scientist
C590. Special education administrator
C591. Special forces officer
C592. Speech pathologist
C593. Speech writer
C594. Sport psychologist
C595. Entertainment agent
C596. Sports agent
C597. Sports physician
C598. Sportswriter
C599. Stained glass artist
C600. Steel worker

C601. Student admissions administrator
C602. Student affairs administrator
C603. Student financial aid administrator
C604. Substance abuse counselor
C605. Subway conductor
C606. Surgeon
C607. Surgical technician
C608. Survey researcher
C609. Surveying technician
C610. Switchboard operator
C611. Systems accountant
C612. Systems analyst
C613. Tax accountant
C614. Tax auditor
C615. Tax collector
C616. Tax examiner
C617. Tax lawyer
C618. Taxi driver
C619. Chauffeur
C620. Teacher of the blind
C621. Teachers' aide
C622. Technical illustrator
C623. Espionage intelligence agent
C624. Textile designer
C625. Tour guide
C626. Town clerk
C627. Traffic administrator
C628. Traffic agent
C629. Traffic technician
C630. Transportation attendant
C631. Travel agent
C632. Travel clerk
C633. Travel counselor
C634. Travel writer
C635. Corporate treasurer
C636. Treatment plant operator
C637. Tree trimmer
C638. Truck driver
C639. Lobby attendant
C640. Veterinarian
C641. Veterinarian technician
C642. Veterinary assistant
C643. Video engineer

C644. High school vocational education teacher
C645. Middle school vocational education teacher
C646. Voice pathologist
C647. Waiter
C648. Waitress
C649. Watch repairer
C650. Weather observer
C651. Welder
C652. Wildlife biologist
C653. Writer
C654. Author
C655. Zoo veterinarian
C656. Zoologist
C657. Road cleaner
C658. Gymnast
C659. Maid
C660. Butler

D. WHAT CIRCUMSTANCES WAS THE VICTIM IN?

D1. In heavy debt
D2. With a penchant for beautiful women
D3. With marriage problems
D4. With a gambling problem
D5. With a secret
D6. With a strange habit
D7. Who keeps odd hours
D8. Who recently came into an inheritance
D9. Who owes money
D10. With family trouble
D11. With a family secret
D12. With a troubled past
D13. Who was having a love affair
D14. Who was having work problems
D15. Who was facing relationship problems
D16. With a secret obsession
D17. With money issues
D18. Who was being stalked
D19. With a dark past
D20. Who likes to keep to himself/herself
D21. On the brink of success
D22. In the middle of a scandal
D23. Who was being laid off
D24. Who was about to be promoted
D25. Embroiled in a corporate scandal
D26. Facing a lawsuit
D27. In deep depression
D28. In a career rut
D29. Who lied about his/her past
D30. About to expose his/her boss
D31. With a mysterious past
D32. With a mysterious family background
D33. With a dark family past
D34. With a dark family secret
D35. Covering up for somebody
D36. Going through a divorce
D37. Facing a divorce
D38. Who was fired recently
D39. Who lost a lot of money

D40. Who lost all his/her money
D41. Being blackmailed
D42. With a shady past
D43. With links to the mafia
D44. With a perverse hobby
D45. Involved in shady business
D46. Who was being threatened
D47. With a penchant for wine
D48. With a penchant for fast cars
D49. Who stole something
D50. Who blew the whistle on his/her employer
D51. Who betrayed his/her family
D52. Who betrayed his/her country
D53. Who betrayed his/her spouse
D54. Who was two-timing his/her girlfriend/boyfriend
D55. Who was a spy
D56. Who was a corporate spy
D57. Who was engaged in corporate espionage
D58. Who was spying on someone
D59. Who was hiding something
D60. With close relations to the mafia
D61. With close relations to the government
D62. Who was harbouring a criminal
D63. Whose entire life was a lie
D64. Who is not what he/she seemed to be
D65. Who does something odd every night
D66. Who does something strange every morning
D67. With a peculiar habit
D68. Who does something peculiar every afternoon
D69. Who does something odd every week
D70. Who visits somewhere odd every evening
D71. Who does something strange every day
D72. With a strange tattoo on his/her body
D73. With bizarre markings on his/her body
D74. Who was blackmailing somebody
D75. Who was hiding something
D76. Who had seen something he/she shouldn't
D77. Who was an important court witness
D78. Who was holding onto an important document
D79. Who possessed a crucial piece of evidence
D80. Who lied to his/her family
D81. Who lied to his/her employers
D82. Who held the key to a secret

D83. Who lied to his/her spouse
D84. Who was hiding something that happened two decades ago
D85. Who was disfigured in a terrible accident years ago
D86. Who was rumoured to be of royal lineage
D87. Who was leading a double life
D88. Who was involved in a robbery heist a decade ago
D89. Who was planning to flee the country that night
D90. With a fatal love
D91. Who is an alcoholic
D92. Who is an ex-CIA agent
D93. Who was an undercover agent
D94. Who was an undercover journalist
D95. Who was an ex-convict
D96. With a grudge
D97. With enemies
D98. With a jealous rival
D99. With a rival at work
D100. Who was acquitted from a crime some years ago
D101. Who was a victim of domestic abuse some years ago
D102. With a reputation for womanizing
D103. Who had undergone plastic surgery
D104. Who had an affair with his/her boss
D105. Who likes to brag
D106. With a fetish
D107. Who was involved in a scandal with a politician
D108. Living with his/her musician boyfriend
D109. Who was having a love affair with a student
D110. About to reveal something to the press
D111. Having multiple love affairs
D112. Cheating on his/her spouse
D113. About to release a research paper
D114. About to break into the limelight
D115. Who was involved in a domestic abuse case some years ago
D116. In the middle of a sex scandal
D117. With intense rivalries at work
D118. About to retrench the staff
D119. With a penchant for vintage cars
D120. Who lied about something
D121. Who found something suspicious
D122. Who discovered a secret
D123. Who overheard a secret
D124. Who was on the run
D125. About to go to the police

D126. From a wealthy family

D127. On holiday

D128. Who suspected his/her girlfriend/boyfriend of cheating on him/her

D129. Who suspected his/her spouse of cheating on him

D130. Who was going to unveil his/her research findings

D131. In the midst of deciding his will

D132. In possession of lab secrets

D133. Transporting something illegal

D134. Who was visiting a patient

D135. Who takes bribes

D136. Who was planning to resign

D137. With designs on his/her parents-in-laws' wealth

D138. With designs on his/her spouse's wealth

D139. Who was acquitted of a criminal case some years ago

D140. Who took bribes

D141. About to reveal an important find to the press

D142. Who likes to drink heavily

D143. Who had gone missing a week ago

D144. With jealous rivals

D145. In a family dispute

D146. About to sign a large contract

D147. Who was very ill

D148. Who had designs on his/her child's trust fund

D149. Who was suffering from a terminal illness

D150. Who had been faking his/her family background

D151. Who had been pretending to be rich

D152. Who had no friends

D153. Who was looking for his/her missing spouse

D154. Who was looking for his/her missing child

D155. Whose child recently passed away

D156. Whose spouse recently passed away

D157. Whose parent recently passed away

D158. Who had loaned a large sum of money to a friend

D159. Who was involved in a dispute over child custody

D160. Who had a obsessive compulsive disorder

D161. Who had a multiple personality disorder

D162. About to embark on a boat trip

D163. About to inherit a large sum of money

D164. About to marry

D165. About to divorce

D166. About to get engaged

D167. About to get promoted

D168. Who has a grudge against a family member

D169. Who was being blackmailed by his/her secret lover
D170. Who had threatened to expose his/her boss
D171. Who was smuggling illegal drugs
D172. Who was working for the mafia
D173. Who was holding onto a mysterious item
D174. Who was stalking a celebrity
D175. Who was involved in a domestic dispute
D176. Who had been bullying a colleague
D177. Who had been abusing his/her spouse
D178. Who was not on speaking terms with his/her family
D179. Who was not on speaking terms with his/her spouse
D180. Who was addicted to something
D181. Who was shunned by his/her neighbours
D182. Who had a secret hobby
D183. Who had a history of petty crimes
D184. Who lost all his/her friends
D185. Who recently lost his/her home
D186. Who had recently threatened to kill someone
D187. Who was known to be eccentric
D188. With appeared on the surface to be the perfect spouse
D189. With friends in high places
D190. Who had stolen funds from his/her company
D191. Who was desperately in need of money
D192. Who had mysteriously disappeared two weeks ago
D193. Who had been swindled out of his/her life savings recently
D194. Who was a secret drug addict
D195. Who was disabled
D196. Who was suffering from amnesia
D197. Who had recently been humiliated
D198. Who had recently quarrelled with a friend
D199. Who had recently lost a valuable object
D200. Who had been looking for his/her adopted parents
D201. Who had a strained relationship with his/her brother
D202. Who had gambled away money entrusted to him/her
D203. Who had recently fallen on hard times
D204. Who had been sleeping on the streets
D205. Who had a volatile relationship with his/her sister
D206. Who was estranged from his/her mother
D207. Who had been bickering with his/her father
D208. Who was not on good terms with his/her colleague
D209. Who was known to be hostile to his/her neighbour
D210. Who had cut off all contact with his/her children

E. WILD CARD DETAIL

E1. A witness had seen the victim quarrelling with someone
E2. A witness had heard a strange noise
E3. The victim had left behind a note
E4. The victim's shoes are missing
E5. The victim had unexplainable bruises on his/her leg
E6. The victim had strange bruises on his/her foot
E7. The victim has a burn mark on his/her shoulder
E8. The victim's hand was tied behind his/her back
E9. The victim's wrists show signs of being tied
E10. There was no sign of a struggle
E11. A witness is lying
E12. A witness had seen the victim behaving fearfully the day he/she died
E13. The victim's clothes are wet
E14. The victim's hair is wet
E15. The victim's hands are wet
E16. Something is abnormal about the victim's hand
E17. There is something suspicious about a stain on the victim's leg
E18. There is something strange about the victim's clothing
E19. The victim's clothes are missing
E20. Something is missing from the victim's clothes
E21. The victim was trying to reach something
E22. The victim died in an unusual posture
E23. The victim had unexplainable bruises on his/her forearm
E24. The victim held a torn piece of paper in his/her hand
E25. The victim had left behind a curious message
E26. A witness has tampered with the murder scene
E27. The victim's hair is sticky with something
E28. There is a white substance on the victim's fingers
E29. There is some sort of powder on the victim's shoes
E30. The victim's mobile phone has a secret message
E31. A witness has heard the murderer's voice
E32. Something is wrong with the victim's estimated time of death
E33. There is a deep cut on the victim's lips
E34. The victim's ankles were duct taped together
E35. The victim has a burn mark on his/her leg
E36. The victim had scratched a message before he/she died
E37. The victim had left behind a bizarre message on his/her mobile phone
E38. A witness saw the victim running out of his/her home
E39. A witness saw the victim chasing after someone
E40. A witness heard the victim scolding somebody
E41. The victim's belt is missing

E42. Something is missing from the victim's belongings
E43. The victim's glasses are missing
E44. The victim was wearing only one contact lens
E45. There are strange marks on the victim's wrists
E46. There is a odd smudge at the victim's neck
E47. The victim's tie is tied the wrong way
E48. The victim's shirt is tucked the wrong way
E49. A button is missing from the victim's coat
E50. The victim's fingernails have an unidentified substance underneath them
E51. The victim was grabbing at something before he/she died
E52. The murderer had left behind a clue on the victim's skin
E53. Someone saw the victim dashing out of his/her office
E54. The victim was wearing shoes that do not belong to him/her
E55. The victim's wedding ring is missing
E56. Someone saw the victim in an unexpected place before he/she died
E57. There is a strand of hair in the victim's hand
E58. A witness saw the victim shouting at someone
E59. The victim had strange bruises on his/her arm
E60. The victim's hair band is missing
E61. A witness saw the murderer's back view
E62. A missing key is involved
E63. An inheritance will is suspected of being forged
E64. A piano wire is found on the scene.
E65. A lipstick mark was found on the victim's shirt
E66. The victm's footprints stopped twenty feet away from the body
E67. The victim's home was ransacked
E68. The victim's ankle has a thin red line on it
E69. The victim's eyes were dilated
E70. There are red spots on the victim's neck
E71. There is a strong scent in the crime scene
E72. The room of the crime scene was unusually hot
E73. The victim was blindfolded
E74. There is a bloodstain at the doorway of the crime scene
E75. There is a black mark on the victim's fingernail
E76. A torn scarf is found near the crime scene
E77. Someone had videotaped the murder
E78. The victim's hands were tied together with vines
E79. The soles of the victim's shoes are muddy
E80. The victim's wrist watch stopped at midnight
E81. The victim's hand seemed to be pointing at something
E82. There was a ransom note stuffed in the victim's pocket
E83. Someone witnessed the victim tearing up an envelope furiously

E84. A witness noticed the victim in tears the day before

E85. A page is torn from the victim's diary

E86. The victim's forearm has tiny needle marks

E87. The lock to the victim's home was broken

E88. The victim's mouth was stuffed with leaves

E89. A witness overheard the victim having an angry phone conversation with someone

E90. There is adhesive residue on the victim's fingertips

E91. The victim's watch is missing

E92. The room of the crime scene was unusually cold

E93. There is a tiny spot of blood on the victim's forehead

E94. An arrow is found some distance away from the crime scene

E95. A broken off key was found at the crime scene

E96. The murder took place in the heat of summer

E97. The murder took place in the dead of winter

E98. A glove is missing from the victim's hand

E99. There is a torn hole in the victim's trousers

E100. The victim's shirt pocket was ripped off

E101. There are strange marks on the victim's eyelids

E102. There was a hastily written note stuffed in the victim's pocket

E103. The victim had received something unusual in the mail before he/she died

E104. The victm's face was bloated

E105. A witness had overheard a strange conversation

E106. The blood splatters on the walls do not match up

E107. The victim held a torn photograph in his hand

E108. A witness saw the victim in a dispute with someone

E109. The back of the victim's neck is sticky with something

E110. The hard disk of the victim's laptop has been erased

E111. The victim received an odd message on his/her mobile phone before he/she died

E112. A witness saw the victim exchanging suitcases with someone on the street

E113. A tattoo on the victim's arm may provide a clue to the murderer's identity

E114. There are red scars on the victim's neck

E115. A thumb drive is missing from the victim's handbag

E116. The victim had hurried out of the house after receiving a strange phone call

E117. The blood splatters on the walls do not match up

E118. There was red ink all over the victim's hands

E119. The victim was going to reveal something important to a witness before he/she died

E120. There is something odd about the cutlery on the table
E121. There is an odd lipstick smudge at the victim's neck
E122. The victim's hands were tied to the steering wheel
E123. The victim's notebook pages are all torn out
E124. Some burnt papers were found in a fire near the crime scene
E125. The victim's ankle has a thin red thread around it
E126. The victim's water was drugged
E127. The room was locked from the inside
E128. Something is missing from the victim's desk
E129. Something is abnormal about the victim's fingers
E130. The victim's hand is tightly clutched together
E131. The victim has a red line on his/her forehead
E132. There are strange cuts on the victim's legs
E133. The murderer had an accomplice
E134. The victim's hand is firmly gripping an object
E135. A witness saw the victim having an intense conversation with someone
E136. The victim's bodice/shirt has a faint stain on it
E137. The victim's feet were tied together
E138. There is a needle mark on the victim's neck
E139. The victim had complained of someone stalking him/her
E140. The victim was tied to the bed
E141. A missing key to a safe is involved
E142. A witness noticed the victim behaving secretively the day before
E143. A witness heard the victim bragging about something
E144. The victim had unexplainable bites on his/her forearm
E145. There is an unidentified powder on the victim's wrist
E146. The victim received a mysterious voice recording before he/she died
E147. Some photos are missing from the victim's briefcase
E148. There was a letter in the victim's pocket
E149. The murderer had left behind a clue on the victim's hair
E150. A burnt locket was found at the crime scene
E151. A witness saw the victim exchanging something with someone in a car
E152. The victim held a broken fan in his/her hand
E153. The victim has a black mark on his/her temple
E154. Someone witnessed the victim beating up someone furiously
E155. The victim made a strange remark before he/she died
E156. Something is missing from the victim's wallet
E157. The victim had unexplainable bite marks on his leg
E158. The victim's neck is mottled
E159. The weather proves to be the murderer's downfall
E160. There was a sound recording of the murder

E161. There were crushed and broken leaves all around the body
E162. A burnt pantyhose was found near the crime scene
E163. A witness heard the murderer's voice
E164. There are marks around the victim's mouth
E165. A lock of hair was found at the crime scene
E166. There is a shattered glass of water beside the body
E167. The body had been dragged for a distance
E168. There was a note pinned to the victim's chest
E169. An envelope is missing from the victim's bag
E170. The victim's car had been ransacked
E171. There is something strange about the victim's socks
E172. There is a cut on the victim's neck
E173. The victim's niece received something in the mail from the victim before he/she died
E174. There is a blue stain on the victim's coat
E175. A stash of secret photos was found in the victim's home
E176. The victim's home was burned to the ground
E177. The victim was gagged
E178. There is something in the victim's mouth
E179. There was a receipt in the victim's pocket
E180. There was a strong smell of alcohol on the victim's body
E181. The victim had suspected his/her spouse of having an affair
E182. There is a black stain on the victim's fingernail
E183. The victim had sent out a message to his/her friends before he/she died
E184. A long line of snapped thread is found at the crime scene
E185. Two reliable witnesses gave conflicting accounts of the same event
E186. The murderer had dropped a clue near the body in his/her haste
E187. A witness heard the victim boasting about something
E188. Someone received a call from the murderer after the victim was killed
E189. The door of the crime scene was locked from the inside
E190. There is a grey substance on the victim's thumb
E191. The victim's hand is frozen in an odd gesture
E192. The victim's mobile phone was bugged
E193. The victim tore something up before he/she died
E194. All the witnesses have something to hide
E195. A secret cipher is involved
E196. The victim had left behind a coded message
E197. The victim was going to meet a private investigator
E198. Someone witnessed the victim destroying a tape recording
E199. There was a map in the victim's pocket
E200. The victim's clothes are oily with something
E201. A witness noticed the victim in distress the day before

E202. A family member noticed the victim in distress the day before
E203. The victim had been dead for over a month
E204. A broken bit of plastic is found near the crime scene
E205. The blood splatters on the ground do not match up
E206. The victim was suffering from a nose bleed
E207. A twisted ring was found at the crime scene
E208. There was something smeared on the victim's forehead
E209. There was a red thread tied around the victim's wrist
E210. There was a smear of ink on the victim's hand
E211. The victim brushed past someone suspicious before he/she died
E212. There is a strong smell at the crime scene
E213. A witness saw the victim speaking to someone in a car
E214. There is a rip in the victim's pants
E215. The victim had left a strange message on his/her phone the day he/she died
E216. There are scratches on the victim's hands
E217. The murderer had left behind a clue on the victim's lips
E218. There was something strange about the way the victim held the cutlery
E219. A charcoal mark was found on the victim's shirt
E220. The murder took place after closing hours
E221. A body part is missing
E222. There are red scratches on the victim's desk
E223. A witness is concealing important evidence
E224. A witness had seen the victim behaving strangely the day he/she died
E225. There is a cufflink missing from the victim's clothes
E226. There were crushed glass pieces all around the body
E227. The victim held a torn ticket in his hand
E228. A torn jacket is found near the crime scene
E229. The victim was drugged
E230. Secret documents was found in the victim's laptop
E231. A burnt dog collar was found near the crime scene
E232. There are red scratches on the victim's face
E233. There is something odd about the victim's wardrobe
E234. There is an oily residue on the victim's fingertips
E235. A broken watch was found at the crime scene
E236. There were bits of glass around the body
E237. Someone witnessed the victim berating someone furiously
E238. The victim's shirt buttons were ripped off
E239. A thumb drive is missing from the victim's pocket
E240. A witness noticed the victim in a panic the day before
E241. The victim's shoelace is missing
E242. A frayed rope is found at the crime scene

E243. A witness saw the murderer's hand
E244. There was a strong smell of perfume at the crime scene
E245. A witness heard the victim complaining about something
E246. The victim was wearing a winter jacket in the hot weather
E247. The victim was wearing very little in cold weather
E248. The victim's tie has a large hole in it
E249. There are clay marks on the victim's earlobes
E250. The victim had been dead for over a week
E251. A dirty handkerchief was found at the crime scene
E252. The victim's fingers were chopped off
E253. A witness saw the murderer's masked face
E254. The victim has a bruise on his/her shoulder
E255. There are clay marks on the victim's heels
E256. There was a twist of red paper in the victim's hand
E257. The victim had been dead for over a decade
E258. An inheritance will is involved
E259. A paw print was found near the body
E260. There is an odd smudge at the victim's neck
E261. The victim held a torn bit of cloth in his hand
E262. The victim's uniform has an odd stain on it
E263. The victim had been dead for over a year
E264. There is a rip in the victim's shirt
E265. The victim died pointing to something on the wall
E266. The victim scrawled a message before he/she died
E267. A witness saw the victim speaking secretively to someone
E268. Someone witnessed the victim destroying some papers
E269. Something is abnormal about the victim's mouth
E270. The victim has a bruise on his/her forearm
E271. The victim's hands were tied behind his/her back
E272. The victim's shirt has a faint stain on it
E273. There was blood in the victim's mouth
E274. A long coil of rope was found at the crime scene
E275. Evidence of the murderer's crime on his/her clothes
E276. A witness unwittingly helps the murderer escape
E277. The ceiling contains evidence pointing to who the murderer was
E278. There are multiple murderers in this murder
E279. A witness betrays the murderer
E280. The murderer is a family member of the victim
E281. A broken kite string is found at the crime scene
E282. An opened bottle of pills was found at the crime scene
E283. The victim's handkerchief was found in a nearby trash bin
E284. The victim's body showed burn marks
E285. The victim was wearing the wrong watch

E286. The air conditioning at the crime scene was set unusually cold
E287. There was a blackout when the victim was killed
E288. The victim had been lured out of his/her home by someone familiar
E289. The murderer had disguised himself as a police officer
E290. The victim had a string of lovers
E291. A lighter was found at the crime scene
E292. The victim had snapped a blurry photo of the murderer before he/she died
E293. A witness is trying to frame an innocent person
E294. A witness is trying to mislead the investigation
E295. There is blood at the crime scene that does not belong to the victim
E296. All the witnesses are lying
E297. A child had witnessed the murder
E298. A broken bangle was found at the crime scene
E299. The victim's pendant was missing
E300. A message had been spray painted onto the victim's body

Thank You

For Reading "500 Mystery Murder Scenes For Writers"

If you enjoyed this book or received value from it in any way, then I would like to ask you for a favor. Would you be kind enough to leave a review for this book on Amazon? It will be greatly appreciated!

ABOUT THE AUTHOR

Irin Blackburn is a writer, history lover and dedicated purveyor of crime news and mysteries. A collector of odd facts and stories related to crime and murder mysteries, she is always on the lookout for new inspirations for crime and murder mystery writers.

Printed in Great Britain
by Amazon